Praise for *Building a Better Nest*

"Reading Evelyn Hess is like sitting with friends around a campfire on a chilly autumn night, hands wrapped around a warm mug of tea, staring into the flames while listening to a good story. Hess's level-headed, open-hearted encounters with the world remind us of our responsibility to be good neighbors to everything in nature. *Building a Better Nest* is quietly eloquent and plainly wise."

—Charles Goodrich, author of *The Practice of Home*

"Evelyn Hess's nests—family history, the house she and her husband are building, their 21 foothill acres, and the greater house of nature—fit one-in-the-other not as neatly as Russian dolls. There are obstacles, cross-purposes, disappointments, small disasters, and she learns from every one. She is living an audacious, lifelong, deeply conscious journey into self and place—or better, into self in place. Many of us share her values but lack her gumption."

—John Daniel, author of *Rogue River Journal* and *Of Earth: New and Selected Poems*

"Hess's respect and love for the earth is palpable as she recounts her journey of creating a sustainable home, mindful of the impact on her planetary family each step of the way. She indeed builds a better nest as she guides us through a captivating tapestry of familial, cultural, and economic history—each story adding to and strengthening the integrity of her own nest. Hers is an empowering example of living with awareness and humility at any age and stage of life."

—Mary Christina Wood, author of *Nature's Trust*

C·5

building a better nest

*living lightly at home
and in the world*

EVELYN SEARLE HESS

Oregon State University Press   Corvallis

The paper in this book meets the guidelines for permanence and durability of the Committee on Production Guidelines for Book Longevity of the Council on Library Resources and the minimum requirements of the American National Standard for Permanence of Paper for Printed Library Materials Z39.48-1984.

Library of Congress Cataloging-in-Publication Data

Hess, Evelyn Searle.
  Building a better nest : living lightly at home and in the world / Evelyn Searle Hess.
    pages cm
  Includes bibliographical references and index.
   ISBN 978-0-87071-805-2 (original trade pbk. : alk. paper) — ISBN 978-0-87071-806-9 (e-book : alk. paper)
1. House construction—Oregon—Oregon Coast Range—Popular works. 2. Sustainable living—Oregon—Oregon Coast Range. 3. Hess, Evelyn Searle—Homes and haunts—Oregon—Oregon Coast Range. I. Title.

  TH4815.H47 2015
  690'.837097953—dc23

                    2015012995

OSU
Oregon State
UNIVERSITY
OSU Press

Oregon State University Press
121 The Valley Library
Corvallis OR 97331-4501
541-737-3166 • fax 541-737-3170
www.osupress.oregonstate.edu

In love and gratitude to my grandparents, Jessie Bereman and Burton Leonard Searle, and Stella Barnard and Charles Thomas Yeatts; my parents, J. Dorman and Amy Yeatts Searle, and my husband David Hess; with love, appreciation and blessings for the future to our children, Erika and Jeff Hess, our grandchildren, Nate Hess, Celina Johnson-Hess, Tasha Hess-Neustadt, and Camila Hess-Neustadt, and great grandchildren Evangeline and Benjamin Johnson-Hess.

Contents

Acknowledgments

It takes a village to launch a life, a house, a book. Among the multitude of people for whom I am immeasurably grateful are those who built my first nest: my ancestors, my first family, my teachers, and my childhood friends;

those who contributed physically or materially to the building of our current nest: Curtis Williams and his excellent crew, Ed Van Winkle, Ginny Alfriend, Sandra and Fred Austin, Danny Bellissimo, Jim and Cindy Beyer, Mark and Val Bloom, Howie Bonnett, Stan and Joan Cook, Judith Fernandez, Rachel Foster, Hannah and Dan Goldrich, Roger Gossler, Erika Hess, Jeff Hess, Nate Hess, Judi Horstmann, Anita and Art Johnson, Celina Johnson-Hess, Geoffrey Johnson, Kit Kirkpatrick, Tom LeCascio, John Moriarty, Marietta and Ernie O'Byrne, Nick Otting, Linda Rees, Kate Reinke, Sandra Rossi, Linda and Martin Sage, Keith Stanley and Hilda Ward;

those whose writings gave information and inspiration: Shannon Elizabeth Bell for *Ironweed*, Robert Browning for *Rabbi Ben Ezra*, Gardeners and Farmers of Terre Vivante for *Preserving Food without Freezing or Drying*, Daniel Goleman for *Destructive Emotions: A Scientific Dialogue with the Dalai Lama*, Joseph Jenkins for *Humanure*, Sandor Elliz Katz for *Wild Fermentation* and Sim Vander Ryn for *The Toilet Papers;*

those who gave generously of their time, support, advice or inspiration toward the genesis and completion of *Building a Better Nest*: Cecelia Hagen, Barbara Engel, Quinton Hallett, Patty Jacobs and Barbara Walker; Chantal Gaboriau, and Ernie and Marietta O'Byrne; John Daniel, Charles Goodrich, Kathleen Dean Moore, Marianne Ober, Scott Slovic, and Mary Wood; Mary Elizabeth Braun, Marty Brown, and Micki Reaman of OSU Press; and Nathan E. Hess for my website.

From the beginning to the end, infinite gratitude to my first reader, sustainer, and friend; my architect, my husband, David.

Introduction

After sixteen years of camping on our woodland property in the Oregon Coast Range foothills, David and I were finally ready to build a house. We wanted to apply the lessons of those years of simple living to lives in a more permanent structure, yet, both by choice and necessity, we needed to build on a limited budget. How could we, within our economic constraints, build a better nest?

And what did that mean exactly, to "build a better nest"? Better how? Better than what? Structurally better than camping, certainly: we would have permanent walls and a roof. Functionally better than the trailer: we would have insulation; there would be room to store things where they would be safe from nesting and nibbling critters; and we'd have a stove, a sink, and a shower. But we wanted "better" on a deeper scale. We wanted to live responsibly. That would require, at the very least, not harming the earth, and ideally, giving back gratefully, both to the planet and to our fellow earthlings.

Still, were we looking through rose-colored glasses? Could ordinary folks actually do anything positive on a global scale? Society seems to expect the next president or technology or some corporate philanthropist to solve the problems of the world, but that hasn't happened yet. Now, as the earth faces rising seas, extreme storms, tenuous supplies of fresh water, widening economic disparity, disappearing species, and political squabbling, we can no longer wait to be rescued by some as-yet-unidentified superhero. It has become essential for us just-plain-folks to figure out how best to live our lives.

David and I started with the things a house could do: make a small footprint on the land, take advantage of natural light and air conditioning, use solar energy, collect rainwater. As we planned and worked on the house, at the back of our minds was always the magnitude of the over-arching problem—the myriad ways that individual actions might affect the biosphere.

Clearly, more than the attributes of a house go into human impact on the earth.

Building a Better Nest explores some of those questions. If Western over-consumption is the primary force depleting resources, exploiting vulnerable countries and their people, and at the same time producing greenhouse gases that warm the atmosphere, what is the reason for that level of consumption and is there any way it can be changed? Where did Western society get the idea that happiness is found in accumulation? Can we answer those who see simple living as deprivation? I knew I felt personally fulfilled by living simply, but I wanted to understand the reason. How is it that people who have less material wealth can be as happy as, or happier than, the more affluent? When we visited our daughter's family in Costa Rica, a relatively poor country, during her husband's sabbatical there, we saw small, colorful houses, often with numerous occupants. Pedestrians were common and buses were jammed. Parades, festivals, singing, and dancing replaced the need for paid entertainment. People were friendly and welcoming even though I couldn't speak their language. The number one "industry" in Costa Rica is environmental tourism, honoring habitats, ecosystems, and the species within, saving for tomorrow the gifts of nature as well as celebrating them today. I was interested to find Costa Rica standing at number one on the Happy Planet Index while the United States is 112th.

The United States will never become Costa Rica, but the happiness of the Ticos (Costa Ricans) should demonstrate that neither having stuff nor being a superpower is a prerequisite to contentment. This is an important point, because there won't be many recruits to simple living if it is deemed to preclude happiness.

As building the house progressed, I decided to turn the investigation inward. Where did I, in the low economic 50 percent, find contentment? And where did I pick up attitudes that help me in that quest? "If you look deeply into the palm of your hand," wrote Thich Nhat Hanh, "you will see your parents and all generations of your ancestors. All of them are alive in this moment." I looked for clues in my own childhood during the Depression, war, and post-war years, and to the lives of my parents and their parents, lives that, in a general way, are backgrounds shared by many of us in this nation. How did they live? What did they learn? How did they change and how did they influence me?

Returning to the question: can an individual make a difference? To me, it seems clear. The world's population is composed of individuals—over seven billion of them, and growing by more than two hundred thousand a day. Making a difference will require a change of attitude from what is common today, perhaps a change of economic system. But if a good percentage of us could find keys to happiness outside of consumption, we could solve some problems, slow others, and learn how best to survive in the damaged world that we have created. If we put our minds and hearts to it, there is still time to save for our posterity some of the natural world that we were born into. I believe a move in this direction is not only possible, but that it is happening right now as more and more people recognize their connections, realize that others share the same feelings and needs, and find ways to communicate and work together for the sake of our sanity, our communities, and our planet.

But now David and I need to turn our attention to the job at hand: stick by stick, straw by straw, building a nest of our own.

I
Preparation

Build, therefore, your own world.
—RALPH WALDO EMERSON

May 2008. The economy is in the midst of a major collapse—the worst in nearly eighty years. Now seventy-two years old and retired, we have a grand total of sixty thousand dollars to our name and are about to begin building a house. Even the weather is a gamble. We can count on only five reasonably dry months before the rain year begins here in the southern end of Oregon's Coast Range foothills.

Are we crazy? Maybe so. But after sixteen years of camping, much of the time planning our "someday house," we are loathe to wait any longer. Our bank balance is clearly meager, but certainly enough to get started. And all we need to do before the rains begin is to get a roof on. As for our age, I don't accept the idea of being "too old" as long as we're upright and the wheels are still turning, whether we are forty-eight, seventy-two, or eighty. My philosophy is that life is for living. If we really want to do something, we ought to get on it whatever age we are.

Still, this age thing is a bit like the weather. I wouldn't refuse to go outside merely because it's snowing, but it would be foolish to ignore the fact of the snow. At the least, I should dress accordingly. Even though David and I have never defined ourselves according to age, we do acknowledge that energy can flag. Backs, knees, and other joints sometimes go on strike. Hearts wear out. We have already out-lived David's father and several of our friends; we're just a few years short of the ages my parents were when they died and our own road to this point has been a circuitous one, filled with potholes and tangled in bramble vines.

For sixteen years, beginning just past our fifty-seventh birthdays in December 1992, David and I camped in a tent or an old trailer without frivolities such as running water and electricity. A few years earlier we had bought these twenty-one acres of hilly woods southwest of Eugene for our plant nursery. After a delightful summer camping here, we knew we could manage without amenities, so when we needed to extract ourselves from a financial hole we had climbed into during the recession of the eighties, a move seemed the obvious solution. We would rent out our house near the university and camp on our beautiful land in the hills.

We made the move. We worked our nursery on the land, designed and installed gardens in town, counted stars, and listened to coyotes howl at night. Just over two years into our venture came the first major pothole, one that seemed more like plunging over a cliff at the time.

When he was fifty-nine, David had a massive cerebral hemorrhage. He survived brain surgery, but his life was in the balance for weeks and the quality of his future remained a question for much longer. The gaunt fellow with the shaved head and fixed gaze who eventually emerged from the hospital had little in common with my curly-haired architect husband. His mathematical ability and spatial sense were all but gone, and it was a good five years before he was able to draw much more than a lopsided triangle.

But David gradually made his way back to health and function. Motivated by the need for medical insurance, I spent a couple of years working for the city, gardening in Eugene's first park, a beautiful rhododendron garden, at the same time continuing to grow the nursery plants that, once he was well enough, David sold. To the tune of the seasons and the songs of birds and crickets, we hauled water by day and lit the night with headlamps and candles, while clothes moldered in the trailer and mice used them for nests. Through it all, we got reacquainted with each other and learned to communicate on a deeper level.

Those years were as rewarding as they were instructive and challenging. I felt his return to life was an enormous gift; when he retrieved our old house plans and was able once again to see them with an architect's eyes, it seemed a complete miracle. As David's drawings progressed, I was eager to realize his vision, and I felt considerable urgency: we needed to do it quickly, while we were in reasonably good health and still had a few pennies in the bank. For what might tomorrow bring?

In fall 2001, after David finished our house plans, he took them to the county and wrote a check to get a building permit. The first step to a real house! I was practically hyperventilating with excitement. Probably David was happily expectant as well, though he didn't show it. I saw only the routine, professional way he had proceeded for so many years in his architectural practice. But then we hit the next bump.

We hadn't realized that the building permit was the *last* of several steps we had not yet climbed, the first of those being to request a land-use permit—a petition to the county for the right to build a house on this particular piece of rural land. Of course we knew such things were necessary, but we were so caught up in the design process and the possibility that our long-held dream might actually come true that we didn't think it through. Trying not to let our spirits deflate, we got the requisite forms and began our research. But deflate they did, and we allowed ourselves to get seriously sidetracked from pursuing the land-use permit. In the late summer of 2006 we finally submitted the request and in February 2007, five months later and six years after David first delivered our building plans, the county agreed that we could move forward.

The examiners won't even look at the building plans, though, until other requirements have been met: The driveway must be approved (six inches of packed rock at least twelve feet wide, with a minimum of fourteen feet of overhead clearance). A fire break of thirty feet needs to be cleared around the house, plus an additional 150 feet with tree canopies no closer than fifteen feet apart. A septic system must be installed.

Some of our country friends wonder why we even bother with a building permit. Sometimes I wonder too, when we have to fork out another few hundred dollars we don't have to spare, or accommodate a regulation that conflicts with our plans. Maybe it is because we were forties and fifties kids. Good, don't-rock-the-boat kids. Worship-at-the-feet-of-the-professor kids. But even so, we really do believe in land-use laws. Folks shouldn't be able to make roads and build houses willy-nilly, wherever the spirit moves them.

So we chop the branches off two trees fresh-cut from the stand of skinny firs growing dense as hog hair over our hillside. Then, David and I walk the long driveway. I hold my fourteen-foot fir pole straight up to measure clearance beneath branches that overhang the drive, while David carries his twelve-foot pole crossways, measuring the driveway's width. Any vegetation breaching that fourteen-foot sacred space loses its head. *Thwack!* And any within the prescribed twelve-foot width, we grub out. We walk from the house site toward Easy Acres Drive, the road that leads to Territorial Highway, then north to Veneta, south to the community of Lorane, or east on Lorane Highway to Eugene, twenty miles northeast of us.

The spot we have in mind for our house sits on the brow of the hill that our driveway circumscribes. It is part of an old logging skid-road, one of few level strips on the south-facing slope of this bump of Coast Range foothills. As you head from the house site toward the road, the driveway is a slash in the steep hillside. The hill rises quickly to the left, covered with second-growth Douglas firs interspersed with white oaks and an occasional dogwood. Patches of fawn lily and wild iris paint cream and purple splashes from April to June. To the right the land plunges down through young oaks, big-leaf maples, and dogwoods to the neighbor's green pasture. Beyond, you see the arrow-straight ribbon of Territorial Highway shooting due south. Coyote Creek is down there too, wending its way through the bottomland, but we can't see it from here. It makes its presence known farther north in fall and winter, when, during a heavy rain, it escapes its banks and claims the roadbed as its own.

Earlier we had our friend Bruce, from Lorane's B&B Excavating, re-grade this quarter-mile section of our drive between the house site and the road, adding twenty yards of new gravel. Now we prune and grub, wheel-barrow additional loads of gravel, rake, and measure again. If it's more than twelve feet solid and clear, our procession of two moves on.

Though we work through the spring and summer supplementing and tidying the driveway, clearing brush and cutting trees for the firebreak, I drag my feet, forgetting that at our age, time matters. I'm not keen on cutting all those trees. I moved to the woods because I wanted to live in the woods, not in a clear-cut. I worry about spending so much money on a driveway; and I really don't want the septic either.

Some years ago, Marston, an architect friend, shared pictures from the Middle East, where he had worked and traveled. I was quite taken with the sunrise-colored landscape. All of the buildings and the desert itself were washed in the same red-gold glow. As I admired the warm monotones, I noticed that each home had at least one tall chimney. *Curious*, I thought. *With nary a tree nor any other wisp of green in sight, what could they be burning? Coal? Oil?*

Marston explained that those stacks were not chimneys for fireplaces, but vents for bathrooms. Composting toilets wasted no scarce desert water; any fumes disappeared up the flue; and once composted, nutrients from the residue could be recycled for fertilizer. He said he never noticed any odor.

How simple and wise! Water is getting to be the planet's most limited resource. Whoever came up with the supposedly civilized notion of using water—clear, clean drinking water—to transport human metabolic waste to be treated (or not) and dumped in the river didn't have a very clear crystal ball.

Now many people realize that high organic deposits, such as fertilizer or the contents of sanitary sewers, disrupt and destroy ocean ecosystems. They know water must be conserved; nutrients must be recycled; and that most fertilizer is manufactured from petroleum products. Yet in our urine alone, each of us produces about a quart a day of combined nitrogen, phosphorous, potassium, carbon and calcium, plus trace elements. And each day, tons of that potential fertilizer, along with hundreds of thousands of gallons of water, are flushed away. On average, each American flushes up to thirty gallons of water a day down the toilet—close to half of her daily water use. I began researching how to construct composting toilets and how to use the compost safely.

So why are we planning to install a septic tank and drain field?

Because that's the way it's done in Lane County. Because my retired-architect husband doesn't feel comfortable designing a composting system. Because the county planners won't even look at the building plans until the septic has been installed. So I mutter and mumble, and begin planning an outdoor composting privy, perhaps down near the garden, and look forward to the day when the necessity of recycling this most basic of human products informs codes, technology, and social understanding.

It's already September of 2007 and, clearly, the septic work must be done while the ground is still parched from our typically dry summer. Rain is sure to come soon: maple leaves are turning gold, and fiery scarlet poison oak already clothes dark tree trunks. The septic company's heavy machinery would damage wet soil, and wet soil would make the work dangerous.

We'd best just follow the instructions and not dally. We've already waited six years to progress toward getting a building permit; in another six years, we'll be pushing eighty if we're still around. The clock is ticking.

And so David and I let the big machines loose on the hillside. The crew installs three lines of leach-field pipe, totaling about four hundred feet, then they dig a hole nearly big enough to bury a VW beetle, and in it, install a thousand-gallon septic tank. I see the mess they are making on the slope and bite my tongue, acknowledging the exigency of the project and appreciating that the men are knocking back the non-native blackberries that seem to resurrect as fast as we try to remove them.

Soon the septic system is in and approved. We still have to get the county's okay on the firebreak and the drive, but it's too late in the season to start house construction. So we continue to cut and clear, gravel and trim, moving along the drive with our skinny tree trunks, measuring driveway width and overhead clearance, pruning, making room for the passage of a fire truck that we hope we never have to call.

Two things happen that allow me to relax about cutting trees for the firebreak. The first is an unexpected benefit of our slow and stumbling progress: a year after we begin, the rules soften a bit. Members of our local Audubon Society have convinced the county of the importance of underbrush and a diversity of trees as habitat for wildlife. Of course we still need to clear near the house, particularly on the downhill side. It would be irresponsible (as well as illegal) not to have adequate defensible space. We don't want any firefighters risking their lives because of our carelessness. Both because of the draft that fires create and the fact that they preheat the fuel on the leading edge, fires rage uphill, traveling five to ten miles an hour. Downhill, fires move at only two to three miles an hour. So the best way to protect the house from a wildfire is to remove the fuel below the house. But requirements for other areas are now less stringent, asking only that we thin, not remove, trees and brush beyond the thirty-foot space we must clear around the house.

The second nudge is realizing the importance of reestablishing oak woodlands. When pioneers first came to Oregon, fir trees grew mostly high on hills surrounding the valley. Oak savanna and wetlands dominated the lowlands, and oak woodlands clothed lower hillsides. Native people maintained the open ecosystems through frequent burning, a practice ended by the pioneers. Without the fires, fir trees multiplied, crowding out the oaks and their dependent communities. So I begin spotting firs that are shading the oaks from the south sun. As long as they are not old grandmother trees, they can be cut to give the oaks healthier lives. At the same time that we are thinning flammable firs, as required in the firebreak rules, we free the oaks from the fir's competition and assist in the return of an endangered ecosystem. It helps that Matthew Hall, a forester friend, is doing the cutting. Sympathetic to the goal of releasing oaks and restoring their communities, Matthew is careful, felling trees with a minimum of damage to those left standing, and parking his machinery on the road to yard downed logs up the hill. Atypically for logging operations, he doesn't tear up the forest duff. Eventually it is finished. And it looks great.

Before long, a bright red jeep tools up our newly trimmed and widened drive announcing the arrival of Lane County District Number One's fire chief, come to inspect our handiwork. He approves the firebreak as well as the driveway, but tells us that almost all fires in the area start inside the house, not from forest fire. And he wants us to be aware that it will take a good twenty minutes to get a fire truck from the station to our place, in which time "the house could be a pile of ashes."

Comforting.

2

Mud

Not every soil can bear all things.
—VIRGIL

October's golden days linger; fallen maple and oak leaves carpet the ground with the sweet smell of early decay. We continue sleeping in our tent by the pond and using our outdoor kitchen for as long as weather allows. I would like to stay indefinitely, not relishing a return to the narrow spaces, moldy drawers, and resident mice in the trailer. But return we will to the only solid shelter we have had the past fifteen years, once we are driven inside by wind, rain, and cold.

In November, the rains come with a furious fierceness and we head back to the shack. But I ignore it, keeping my focus beyond its thin walls. Each day I look with increasing anxiety at the place we had carved out of the hillside and leveled off to prepare for house construction. Now rainwater is carrying exposed surface soil down the bank that was cut away on the uphill side of the excavation, forming streams and mud puddles on the house site. I feel a déjà-vu sort of foreboding. Twenty years ago our first major project was an excavation for a pond. Its bank was cut too steep, precipitating the loss of several trees and eventually a slide of soil. In addition, the terrace below the pond, made from excavated soil, turned out to be unstable, slumping from an even, uplifted grade to humps and bumps among meandering rivulets.

As I watch the back part of the house site fill with water, I worry about the bank. Earlier we had noticed a dark V shape in the bank's otherwise yellowish-brown clay. Opinions varied as to its origin: "crappy soil," "old fill from a one-time logging roadway," "shows where it slid before." It turns out to be a source of at least five separate springs birthed when rains come steady and hard, and now it pours with a rush sufficient to take down a raw bank.

Beginning to panic, I pull on my rain gear, grab a shovel, and climb halfway up the steep and slippery bank. The soil soaks and flows and swallows up my boots when I try to re-direct water, even as it continues to gush. "Help!" I holler, and David brings plywood boards for me to stand on, one foot at a time, as I try to stay upright while I wrestle my boots from the mud monster.

I learned in the eighth grade that the *terra* is not necessarily *firma*. I was sitting with friends near the exit of my school's large basement lunchroom in Chehalis, Washington. We were munching our sandwiches, gossiping about our teachers, and sharing scary stories inspired by the movie *San Francisco*, which we had all seen within the week. *San Francisco* dramatically portrayed the 7.0+ magnitude earthquake that split 296 miles along the San Andreas Fault in 1906 and was felt from Oregon to Los Angeles. Sitting in plush seats in our local theater, we heard the rumbling, saw buildings shake and collapse, listened to the people's frantic wails.

Suddenly, as we lunched in the school basement that April day in 1949, windows started rattling and overhead lights began swinging on their long chains. The room grew quiet. Hands stopped halfway to mouths as we stared up at the swinging lights. Then, like a lightning bolt, a crack zigzagged the length of the long wall beside us. The room's eerie silence was broken by screams. Hundreds of girls and boys ran for the steps that would take us outside. I remember grabbing onto the green sweater of the girl in front of me in the midst of a sea of people bounding wildly up the steps.

Since my friends and I had been near the exit, our group was among the first to get outside early enough to see the grass bank between the sidewalk and the road roll and heave like ocean waves. Then someone screamed "my church!" and we all watched the steeple of the Methodist church a block away scatter its bricks like a child's tower of blocks knocked to the ground.

Several of us girls spent the day linked close, arms around each other's waists, semi-hysterical, walking around town viewing broken windows, trees tipped over, cars crushed by collapsed walls. One death was reported in Chehalis, but it was a miracle there weren't more, with likely candidates being junior-high students trampled while stampeding for the door. Forty percent of the local houses and business buildings were damaged, including 1,351 chimneys. The epicenter of this 7.1-magnitude earthquake was between Olympia and Tacoma, about sixty miles north of us. According to the records the ground shook for thirty seconds, though it felt like much longer, and affected 230,000 square miles, including all of Washington, southwest British Columbia, northern Idaho, northwestern Montana, and northwestern Oregon all the way down the coast to Cape Blanco. It was the largest earthquake in the area since European settlement. But statistics aside, my most persistent memory of it through all these years has been the sight of that no-longer-firm ground, bucking and rolling like waves in the sea.

About twenty-five years later, I ran the green plant division for a whole-sale florist and nursery. Every few weeks I enjoyed a visit from Cactus Jack, who delivered flats of cacti in a multitude of shapes and colors. I checked out his offerings, made the day's purchases, and then we caught up on each other's horticultural problems and families' well-being. As he was packing up one day in November, I promised to stop by his nursery on my next trip to Portland. But before I could honor my vow, Bob, a friend from another nursery, told me a harrowing story.

Jack had been on a delivery run to Seattle, his truck loaded with flats of cacti six shelves deep. Bob, also on delivery, drove a few vehicles behind. It was raining hard, as it had been for several days. Near Longview, windshield wipers swishing full speed, with the river to the left and a steep bank to the right, that solid bank turned to mud, its flow burying Jack's truck. Though traffic was delayed for hours, other vehicles were spared. Bob told me that the volume of mud was so fast and dense, it compressed Jack's truck—steel, cacti, and driver—to a pancake little more than a foot thick.

Even within the last decade, the husband of a college friend of mine had thrown on his raincoat and walked into the backyard to check on the hillside behind their northern California house just as a mass of mud rushed down on top of him. By the time rescuers dug him out, it was too late.

So I am well aware that people cannot carve soil at will and expect it to stay put. Eyeing the hill behind the spot where we plan to build our house, I chew my lip and feel my gut constricting. Midway up the bank we'd had a terrace dug, a place to put cisterns that would catch rainwater from our house gutters. Earth-moving machines had taken a bite out of another spot as well, to make space for a root cellar. As the rains, common in this part of the Coast Range foothills, continue beating down, ponds form where the grade leveled for the house foundation tips toward the hill. The hillside behind the root cellar's site sloughs into the ground meant to hold the main-floor area of the house, pushing ponds forward amidst gravel islands. The cistern excavation crumbles into that of the root cellar, carrying soil, chunks of turf, and a rotting log. Excavated soil flows, blocking the natural drainage in front of and beside the house site and pushing yards of liquid clay into the ditch, across the road, and down the hill to an existing temporary stream pouring into the pond, which turns brown. We scrape a path through the mud that crosses the road but can do little to reshape the soil while it is wet and heavy. We will have to wait until the weather dries to solve that problem, if a solution exists.

It's February 2, 2008, and piles of dirty, gravel-pocked snow border the driveway, which is strewn with muddy lichens and bits of Douglas fir, half buried in slush puddles. I walk the path through snowy mud, down to the pond to check the willows, wondering if any of the pussies might pop out and see their shadows on this Groundhog's Day. But they are still so tight in their calyx cradles that it seems unlikely, even if the sun should briefly peek through the clouds. Surely spring is right around the corner—spring, when we can clear the road of mud and get ready for the actual construction of our house. If nothing else goes wrong.

In May we call Daniel, the earth-mover, in hopes that he can remedy the many problems winter revealed. He will dig out a different location for the cisterns on a level spot near the house and at the floor elevation; he'll excavate a wide swale through the woods above the house to intercept surface water coming down the hill, directing it around, rather than toward, the house site; and he'll re-grade the site itself, getting water to flow away from it and down the hill, rather than into it as it now does. Then he will spread four inches of crushed rock over the entire area. Daniel is a big, gentle man, seemingly built to scale for his tracked excavator. He stands hands on hips surveying the mess and intones, "Oh, you guys! Oh, you guys!" But he and his heavy equipment move as gracefully as a dancer, over the house site, up the hill, through the woods. He clearly understands what the problems are and how to solve them. He does a beautiful job.

Then an engineer designs a five-foot-high, sixteen-foot-long wall to be constructed behind the root cellar, strong enough to withstand the force of flowing mud. We hope, with the construction of the new swale, the wall will never be necessary, but we have sufficient respect for the forces of nature to be glad that it will be there.

Now with my attention fixed on the raw part of the bank, where springs still flow during rainy periods, I mentally design reinforcements that will both celebrate the running water and protect the soil. And I gaze at the hill behind the house and imagine its course turned fluid. In spite of my imaginings, I think we're okay. "God willin' and the crick don't rise," as my little sister used to say.

3
The Foundation

Of a good beginning cometh a good end.
—JOHN HEYWOOD

Oceanspray buds are tiny beads by the time Daniel finishes his work. Camas blooms cobalt blue and orange honeysuckle flowers explode from cowl-collar leaves, seducing hummingbirds and butterflies to their nectar. And, seven years after we began the process, the county approves our building permit.

As scattered clouds float by, a wee bird—a vireo—flits through understory shrubs, reaping insects from the branches and making soft *chwee chwee* sounds. I follow its flight to the edge of the woods and lose it. Later I'll search for its hanging, demitasse cup of a nest. A work of fiber artistry, it is woven from leaves, grass, lichen, and moss and lined with fine grass and spider silk, its lips attached to branchlets with grass and more fine, strong, spider webbing. Thinking of it and the chattering babies inside makes my heart sing. And on this day of spring's promise, David begins to build a nest of our own.

He draws a baseline on the foundation plan and establishes its bearing. Using compass, stakes, and string, he then translates that line to the ground. He will act as the general contractor, but if we are going to get a house up and roofed before winter, we need help, at least for building the foundation. Landscape contractor Joe Spivak recommends Curtis, a neighbor, who does excellent work. We give Curtis a call.

Within the week, Curtis drives up in his blue Toyota pickup and hops out, wearing cargo shorts, a brown T-shirt, and hiking boots. A slender, athletic-looking man in his fifties, his dark ponytail threaded in silver, he reaches into the cab, pulls out his tool belt, and buckles it on as he saunters over to the house site. David has borrowed a transit—an optical instrument (basically a telescope with a built-in level) that is used to measure horizontal and vertical angles—from his contractor friend Greg. Now David and Curtis shoot grades with the transit, to be sure the gravel base is billiard-table flat. As I watch David working, I feel a catch in a sharp inhale and my eyes sting. Strong, confident, his curling hair and beard exuberant as the spring day, he in no way resembles my husband of just over twelve years ago. Then comatose, head swaddled in bandages, a pipe protruding from his scalp to vent excessive fluids, he gave little reason for me not to believe the doctor's grave projections for the future. But now, just look at him!

David and Curtis rake gravel as level as possible and tamp it down with a big vibrating compactor. They add more gravel and shoot grades again. Shoot and rake, shoot and rake. I watch the men work and a small voice within me says, *Never give up. Never ever give up on your health, on your dreams, even on the future of this, our earth-home. You are never too old until you think you are. It's not over until it's over.*

Once they know the gravel base is dead level, they begin building forms for the foundation. First they lay 2x8 boards on edge, staking them in place, drawing the house perimeter three-dimensionally on the site. Next they place a second row of boards parallel to and sixteen inches away from the first. Between the boards, three-inch cubes called dobies, set in two lines twelve inches apart, hold steel rods secure and lift them off the ground.

When the men finish for the day, David and I walk through the spaces of this full-scale house plan on the ground so I can rehearse in my mind where each room will be. Say we've been working outside and we come in dirty. We enter by this south-side door, into the mudroom. We can clean up here because it will be plumbed for the washing machine and sink. On this wall we'll have hooks for our rain gear, with a spot for boots below, and over on that wall we'll hang the inverter for solar panels to be installed on our roof, with batteries for the photovoltaic system stored beneath it. Near them, I'll put labeled bins for recycling paper, cans, glass, and plastics. Before we get into the main part of the house, there on our left will be a tiny bathroom, which probably would be what we came into the house for in the first place.

Or maybe we're just getting home from town, or we're greeting guests. (*There's* a concept! Hard to imagine after sixteen years of having no space to ask anyone in, even for a cup of tea.) In that case, we come to the narrow porch and go in the front door over here, on the east side. We enter into a little hall and turn left into the main space. (Had we turned right and opened that door instead, we'd have dropped into the root cellar.) The main floor is a single, open living space, with mudroom and bathroom to the east and the entry area and door to the root cellar to the north, as appendages. The left end (east) of that main space is the kitchen, to the right, the sitting area. David points out where a deck will be, outside the sitting space, on the south side of the house, beside a built-on greenhouse. Upstairs will be the bedroom. As we don't have that dimension yet, we'll explore there another day. But here on the ground level, I walk through the spaces again and again. I find it all incredibly exciting.

The next time Curtis comes, he and David once again shoot grades, this time to be sure the tops of the boards are completely level. Shoot and adjust, again and again. The boards can be lifted and nailed higher on the stakes if need be, or gravel can be scraped away. Then come eighteen-inch square boxes, eight inches deep with steel grids inside, and post-base brackets at the ready. These are for footings to support the posts that will be the beginning of the house's vertical dimension. David has rented a rebar-cutter and bender, a tool that from a distance looks a bit like long-handled loppers mounted on their side, with the top "handle" being a heavy lever that presses down on the rebar to cut it. The men cut about seventy lengths of the reinforcing steel (rebar) and bend them to L shapes, laying them on top of the forms. This will allow us to grab them quickly and insert them vertically in the concrete as soon as it is poured. Finally they begin the forms for the big retaining wall behind the root cellar. This is the wall that the engineer designed to hold back a hillside of mud—the one that is better than drugs to help me sleep at night. For this wall they make the forms of plywood, with a steel grid inside, the vertical rebar sixteen inches apart and the horizontal bars every ten inches. The reinforcing grid for the wall's four-foot base will be laid horizontally. The base will extend eight inches in front and thirty-two inches behind the eight-inch-thick wall, with the back portion buried in soil to increase the wall's stability. When finished, the wall will be five feet tall and sixteen feet long.

At last I get into the act as we prepare to lay perforated drainpipe and eighteen inches of round drainage rock behind the wall. I shove the big flat shovel into the gravel pile, trying to get enough to work quickly, but not so much that I tweak my back. Shovel, lift, twist, and dump it in the wheelbarrow. Many, many loads. Many lifts. Many twists. And many trips pushing the heavy wheelbarrow up the drive from the gravel pile to the drainage ditch. The wheelbarrow tips from side to side and I wonder if its frame will support the weight. Then I wonder how my own frame will hold up. I am so eager to be part of the house building that I am determined to get the job done, but taunted not-so-subtly by my knees and back, I rejoice that we are tackling this job before we're much older. And I remind myself that Dr. Oz says the magic ingredient to healthy aging is exercise.

Once I have a base of a few inches of gravel, I bring out the builder's level. To be sure the water flows through the pipe, we need a slight drop—a quarter inch to each ten feet—that I will acquire by adding or removing gravel. When the grade is correct, we lay perforated pipe, and I cover that with another fifteen inches of gravel. At the end of the day my body feels pummeled and mushed, but my spirits soar. I relish every moment I can be part of the project and acknowledge a bit of a glow that the old bod will still perform.

As I work on the drain line, David and Curtis check and double-check every possible surface. The tops of the form boards must make a level plane. Just as a stable house requires a good foundation, the foundation is dependent on its form boards. The men sight through the transit relentlessly. One spot needs an eighth-inch shim. Shoot more grades. Cross fingers. David grabs a small sprayer from our nursery supplies and sprays diesel oil inside the forms so that the boards can more easily be removed. Then he calls for inspection.

On an unseasonably warm day in June, our son Jeff, our step-grandson Danny, Curtis, David, and I wait nervously for the concrete truck—or am I the only one who is nervous? Mike from Gemini Concrete Pouring arrives with a flatbed full of hoses and a trailer carrying a concrete pump. As he begins setting up, he asks me to go out to the road and look for the "mud" delivery. I am to ask the driver to back the entire quarter mile, all of the way to the construction area from the road, because Mike feels it will be too hard for him to turn around once he gets in. I wait only a few minutes before I see the concrete truck rounding the bend, nearly to our driveway. I give a weak and self-conscious wave, and the driver stops, but the cab is too high for me to see him. So I climb up on the step to the cab and, standing on tiptoes, peek in the window to deliver Mike's request. The enormous truck backs down our narrow curving drive with its load of seven yards of concrete and my stomach is in my throat, imagining him slipping over the edge of a precipitous slope. But the driver is cool and capable, watching his mirrors, maneuvering as if it were entirely routine.

Because it is farthest back, the men decide to start with the retaining wall. Mike clutches the four-inch hose in both hands as it bucks and vomits mud and gravel into the wall's footing. As he begins the sixteen-foot wall, the five of us workers thrust tools into the wet concrete, "puddling" it to release air pockets. We work diligently as Mike moves back and forth along the wall, distributing the flow. The form for the wall is half full when the hose belches out another heavy load. We all gasp in horror and freeze as wet concrete pours out a split in the already multi-braced plywood back. Curtis dashes to repair the form with more bracing but the consensus is that we should abort the wall concrete for the day.

Shaken, we move to more-forward parts of the foundation. As forms are filled, we hurry to help move hoses, to puddle the pours with sticks or shovels, to pull 2x4s over the new pours until the tops are level and smooth, to transport excess concrete on shovels to forms not yet filled, swarming over the site without assignments, just doing what needs to be done. We set the long L-shaped steel bars, short side down, alternating them so they point right, then left, then right again. The locations are pre-marked. They need to be exactly forty-eight inches apart, so each bar will fit through the cell of a concrete block. Each higher course will begin at the center of the block below, to eventually make a four-foot-high foundation wall.

After we finish I look over those vertical steel bars and imagine them as long cuttings in nursery beds. If they would only root and grow canopies, I fantasize, we could set up tents in the orchard-forest. The day is very hot; trees there would be nice.

We hitch a hose to the waterline from the well, sprinkle the concrete three times, and leave it to set.

Oceanspray panicles have loosened, and as we await our second pour a few days later, the first flowers open their tiny stars.

We had thought we'd been careful puddling the retaining wall that first time, but maybe we had been too vigorous. We thought the forms were sturdily built and adequately braced, but they had failed. Now we stand by the newly reinforced wall forms with sticks and shovels ready, barely daring to breathe. Mike puts the J end of the big hose over the top of the form and punches the button to start the pour. Gently, tenderly, we insert our tools to let out pocketed air. We talk in whispers as if we're in a library or church. Thick, gritty, gray concrete begins oozing out of the hose. Mike pours a layer at a time, waiting for the mud to settle between pours. Finally, it reaches the top. Carefully, we smooth it off. If it holds for ten minutes, Mike tells us, it will hold for good. We watch the seconds creep by one by one as if they are old and stiff and arthritic. I stare at the forms, holding my breath.

Finally someone shouts, "All right! We made it!"

As we wait during the next week for the concrete to cure, most of the tiny flowers of the oceanspray open. They flaunt their pistils and stamens, turning the panicles to fluff. Now that it is time to build the foundation wall, Curtis brings in his friend Brad, who from boyhood trained beside his mason father. Willamette Graystone delivers fifteen pallets of plastic shrink-wrapped concrete blocks. Five courses of blocks surrounding the house will require 1,080 blocks. At 40 pounds apiece, that's a total of 43,200 pounds. Yikes!

I am glad it is happening, but don't feel I can be particularly helpful. I'll do better weeding, potting plants, and looking after our granddogs than I would flexing my grossly inadequate muscles, trying to toss blocks around.

Jeff's dog Homer and his then wife Rachel's big red-gold retriever Tiga are with us for the summer while Rachel's house is being readied for sale and the new house is being remodeled. Tiga loves people and greets the builders, leans heavily on them, and then climbs the hill above the construction to sit and bark her orders for the day. Homer, a short-haired, beige and black mixed breed, has always been a bit suspicious of folks he doesn't know, so he circles them anxiously, barking, shying away, and sometimes scaring them as much as he himself is scared. I have a notion that neither the builders nor the project will suffer if the dogs and I vacate for a while, so I turn my back on both the foundation and my plants as Curtis and Brad begin carrying blocks.

I enjoy taking the dogs for walks. They disappear beneath summer's waving grass, their presence distinguishable only by occasional irregularities in the grass's movement, or, if they are near enough, by the rhythmic

Puffer Billy *huh-huh-huh-huh-huh* of their panting. The grass tickles my chin, my nose, my eyebrows. Using the dogs as an excuse, I don't feel guilty for getting out of work.

As we turn to follow a logging road, the dogs flush a grouse that flies low in front of them, bouncing along almost hitting the ground, like a novice pilot making a clumsy landing attempt. Right in front of their noses it zigs and bounces and zags, then turns abruptly to the right and behind the trunk of a Douglas fir. The frenzied dogs, heads down, feet and tails flying, bound up the road and to the tree, pawing at the ground, gazing up the trunk, unaware that the grouse has long since quietly flown across the road and out of sight. A nice lesson in bird brains and dogged determination.

Eventually the dogs and I return and I get back to my neglected garden and nursery work. As I trek up and down the hill the following days, I pause en route to watch progress on the foundation, feeling awe and excitement along with a hollow sensation from my latent dream of building my house with my own hands.

The rebar "cuttings" don't grow as I fancied them doing, but the concrete-block courses do: hot, heavy, exacting work. When the five courses are finished, they will form a forty-inch-high wall above the eight-inch footing. Julia, a lovely, dark-haired young woman, joins the crew. I am delighted to see a woman on the job, feeling that training for this sort of work was a serious lack in my life. David, Curtis, Brad, and Julia mix sand, gravel, and mortar in a rented portable concrete mixer and carry buckets of concrete to fill the cells in the blocks. They set anchor bolts into the wet concrete and drill holes in pressure-treated 2x6 boards as plates to set over the bolts. This, along with the hold-downs (long anchors) on shear walls, holds the house on the foundation, and keeps the walls from wracking in the wind. A very good idea, it seems to me. It had actually never occurred to me that you had to fasten the house to its understructure. No big surprise there, though. There's very little about this house-building business that *isn't* a big revelation to me.

4
Grandfather

No matter how much falls on us, we keep plowing
ahead. That's the only way to keep the roads clear.
——GREG KINCAID

Though I am personally doing little other than gofer jobs on the house, I am learning about the making of a strong and secure foundation—and that gets me thinking about my own foundations. Chances are we would never have been able to begin this house, probably never even have been able to buy the land, without the help of my grandfather.

Burton Leonard Searle, my paternal grandfather, was part of my life from my earliest memory. I got in trouble in fifth grade by answering "six" to the question, "How many are in your family?" The teacher knew I was one of three girls. With two parents, that makes five.

"You can't count your grandfather."

But I knew that I could, in fact, though I didn't argue with my teacher.

I think of him sitting in his big chair, gray hair still thick and wavy in his eighties, suspenders holding up his heavy twill pants, a suit vest over his long-sleeved shirt. He might be listening to Lowell Thomas, Fulton Lewis Jr., H.V. Kaltenborn, or Paul Harvey broadcasting the news on the radio that was as tall as I was. Later there would be the Firestone Hour with Jeanette McDonald and Nelson Eddy calling each other, and the opera on Saturdays. In pensive moments he might put a record on the big hand-cranked Victrola, or play the piano, his bent arthritic fingers still sure on the keys as he sang "September Song" or "Kathleen Mavourneen." Some days he unpacked his violin (I loved watching him rub rosin on his bow) to play instead of sing, frustrated by the aging of his baritone voice.

Often he escaped to his den, a room in an outbuilding located a couple hundred yards below the house on our long acre. The den's walls were papered with pictures of hunting dogs. There he read or wrote letters on his Remington typewriter. I liked to come calling and smell the grandfather smells, which as I now try to conjure, I believe were mostly wool permeated with years of pipe tobacco smoke. I would try to find him in the wall photo of his Omaha National Guard group—five rows of serious-looking young men standing in front of a long, brick building. Their uniforms were reminiscent of the Civil War era, their rifles held like staffs upright beside them. There he was, a few men right of center in the front row. Then I'd put a handful of corn in the grain-grinder mounted on the wall, turn the handle, and make meal to feed the chickens that were housed next door to his den. I was sure the chickens responded to me personally when they came running to their door, rather than to the meal I tossed them.

I can still picture Grandfather chinning himself on the cross bars of the clothesline that stood between the rose garden and rose trellis, and I remember an accidental back somersault as he played tennis on the clay court my parents made by keeping the weeds from growing at the bottom of our narrow acre. I played tennis there a bit myself by junior-high age, but my strongest memories of the court were from years earlier. The clay soil formed large irregular light and dark patches. My big sister, Nancy, and I had made up an adventure game in which the yellow clay was poison. We had to jump from one dark-colored patch to another or we would surely die. We were stranded in the kingdom of an evil ruler, and our sister Beth, then all of two or three, sat patiently on a bench, the captured princess, waiting for us to rescue her. With Nancy and Beth being ten and a half years apart in age, it was one of the only games we three all played together.

I believe Grandfather played a pretty good game of tennis, but I have little memory of it. I have a clear memory, though, of the importance of his pocketknife. I watched him stab slugs with it, cut his fingernails with it, and bring it out again to eat his meals. I also hung around to see him split wood for the wood range and heating stove, and then, on the same stump, chop heads off chickens when their laying days were over. I gazed wide-eyed, feeling a fascinated horror while the headless creatures ran wildly around the chopping block.

My baby sister Beth was born in November of the year I was in first grade. By the time she was three, I would come home from school to see her in a little chair facing Grandfather's big one, a small table in between, the two of them playing poker. They were great companions for each other. As more and more of his old friends died and he became increasingly reminiscent, Beth was the recipient of stories Nancy and I never heard. Unfortunately, young as she was, she remembered few of them in later life.

Grandfather came to live with us when I was just a year old. His wife had died suddenly a couple of years before, and he had no desire to remain on their Montana farm by himself. My father was trying to build a law practice in mid-Depression years; he and my mother had my sister Nancy, who was five-and-a-half years old, and me, age one, and no room in their tiny house in the flood plain. So Grandfather accepted the invitation to live with them with the understanding that he would buy a house with a little land, and he and we four would move there together. All of my life I understood that, in a very real way, our house was his house, and I always considered Grandfather part of my immediate family.

He, on the other hand, had several families. Burton Leonard Searle was born in 1866 in St. Albans, Vermont, into the family of a Methodist minister. He had two older siblings, Alice and Jason, and eventually a baby brother, Charles. When my grandfather was seven, a typhoid epidemic ravaged the area, killing hundreds, including both of his parents. The four orphan children moved to the home of their maternal grandparents, to be cared for by their grandmother and by big-sister Alice, who was then eleven years old.

Three years later, a man named James Dorman and his sister Mary decided that with so many killed in the epidemic, some children must be needing homes. With his friend A. A. Brooks, who I believe was either a relative or in-law of Burton's grandmother, Mr. Dorman visited my grandfather's family and asked young Burton if he would like to go home with him and be his boy. Charlie was too little to leave his grandmother, and Jason, nearly a teenager, was probably considered too old. Ten-year-old Burton felt pride and wonder at being the one selected. He climbed into the buggy, and as the horse headed for Swanton, Vermont, he was determined to measure up.

James and Mary Dorman and their brother Dwight, along with their cousins and Dwight's son Charles, became my grandfather's third family. Their friends and connections became his as well. The Dormans encouraged

Burt's natural penchant for record keeping, found him lessons in violin, piano, and voice, and brought him along on outings to fish, hunt, and sail. If he ever felt nostalgic for his old family, he didn't admit it, though I believe he wrote regularly to Alice and his young brother Charles.

When he was eighteen, Burt moved to Burlington, Iowa, where Dwight worked as a railroad agent, and from Burlington to Omaha, Nebraska, where Charles Dorman helped him get a job with the B&M Railroad. With his railroad income, Burton was able to send money back to Vermont to help Alice, Jason having died by then in yet another epidemic, and once brother Charles was through high school, Burt helped finance his college education.

But at some point in his young-adult life, he had a falling out with his younger brother. As I heard it, he disapproved of Charlie's girlfriend, and Charlie didn't appreciate his counsel. When Grandfather had been with us a few years, we began getting Christmas presents from Uncle Charlie. More years passed, and Grandfather received word that his brother had died, and had left him his stocks. What a confusion of feelings that must have provoked. A fervent New Deal Democrat, Grandfather didn't believe in money speculation. He felt that playing the stock market was greedy, exploitive, and a foolish gamble. But suddenly he owned stocks, courtesy of the brother he had been trying to reconnect with, while at the same time alienating. Now reconciling with Charlie was no longer a possibility, and Grandfather owned stocks he had so disparaged. He never spoke of them through the years, and with the exception of occasional quiet requests of my father ("Could you pick up some cough medicine?")—"medicine" that I discovered Daddy bought for him in bottles at the liquor store—and giving a crisp hundred-dollar bill to each of his three granddaughters at Christmas, he spent little money. Daddy administered the stocks for him through the years and eventually inherited them.

When I was twelve and Grandfather was eighty-one, we heard an urgent thumping on our back door. I'm not sure who was home or who answered the door, but there stood Ray Mercer, our next-door neighbor, with my grandfather in his arms. He had collapsed in the driveway, Mr. Mercer told us, and didn't respond when he went to help him. Our neighbor carried him into the house and laid him on the couch. Grandfather couldn't move, but he was conscious, his intense blue eyes beseeching us to—what? Maybe to make him well, or to explain what had happened. Perhaps it was fear I saw. But I felt those eyes were begging us not to take him to the hospital. Grandfather had rarely been to a doctor, and like many of his generation, considered hospitals places you go to die. But he not only couldn't move, he couldn't speak. And we could at least pretend not to understand the language of the eyes.

St. Helens Hospital was near the junior high, and if I hurried, I could visit Grandfather during the lunch hour and make it back in time for class. One day he greeted me, his excited eyes directing mine to his hand, lying at his side. There I watched his little finger rise, fall, rise, fall. He was thrilled. He had been able to effect and control a muscle response. His brain was in gear, and it could move a finger.

A few days later when I came to visit, his bed was empty. I was shocked and afraid. I thought he had died. *And he'd been improving!* As it turned out, he had indeed improved—enough that he'd gone home. I remember my tremendous relief, but oddly enough, remember little else of his fight back to health. I suppose I was too caught up in my pre-teen dramas to notice, once the crisis had passed and my world was back to normal. Nancy can recall how he painstakingly taught himself to talk. He made or found a chart of the alphabet, pointed to each letter, forced his mouth into the right position, pushed out an attempt at the right sound, and tried again.

In time he did learn to talk, though with a bit of a slur. And he read, listened to the radio, walked a quarter of a mile to get the paper. I don't believe he got back to tennis though, or to chinning himself on the clothesline bar.

Though I remember few details of my grandfather's struggle back from the effects of his stroke, I was sufficiently aware of the results to learn that even if you're down, you don't have to be out. Hard work and determination can alter outcomes. And in retrospect I see that it was that same tenacity, along with a remarkable resilience, that helped him through his life's losses, changes, and challenges.

I grew up and went off to school feeling that Grandfather would forever be sitting in his big chair when I got home. Though always delighted at our homecoming, he was more and more alone among his contemporaries. His wife gone more than two decades, his childhood playmate and lifelong correspondent, cousin Carleton, gone; his dear friend and verbal sparring partner Don Brooks, gone; Emily Waller, longtime correspondent, now also gone. He never met Mrs. Waller, widow of his brother Charlie's college roommate, but I believe he grew to love her and perhaps to dream of visiting his Vermont home with her, through their years of letter writing. When I came home it seemed that Grandfather played *The Last Rose of Summer* a bit more often, and spoke more frequently of being "the last leaf on the tree." I married, and brought home babies, and eventually he was no longer in his big chair.

He was ninety-six when he died.

I didn't see my grandfather during his last few months, leaving me with an unfinished feeling. Perhaps that's why I try to reconstruct his life. Maybe if I can re-create him, I can say a proper good-bye. I'd at least like to tell him that those stocks he reluctantly inherited from Uncle Charlie and passed on to my father were what allowed us to buy our beautiful twenty-one acres, build a pond, and begin to build a house in the Lorane hills.

5

Jessie Knox Bereman Searle

Courage is the most important of all the virtues because without
courage, you can't practice any other virtue consistently.
——MAYA ANGELOU

My grandfather's wife, Jessie Bereman Searle, was always an enigma to me, a mystery I very much wanted to solve. Some photographs from before she was married show an efficient, no-nonsense, professional woman. In one photo, she is one of six women of the Ladies' Cycling Club, all posing beside their bicycles. They all wear hats—Jessie's looks rather nautical—long-sleeved white blouses with big neck bows, leather gloves, and ankle-length dark skirts. In another photo I see an elegant woman, her blond hair piled high, wearing the green taffeta dress with black velvet insets that I lovingly removed from its tissue paper and tried on when I was barely a teen, hoping that the mirror would reflect back to me such glamour. Photos from after she was married show her beside my grandfather, his hair thick and wavy, his generous mustache perfectly groomed, gold chain draped from the vest pocket where he kept his watch. With her in her pleated silk blouse and long dark skirt, the two of them look as if they stepped off the page of a high-fashion magazine. I don't feel that I know her from looking at the photos, but clearly she was a woman of multiple facets and, apparently, self-confident about all of them. Yet in photos from later years, when they lived on their Montana farm, my grandmother sometimes looks strained, tired, resigned.

Jessie was twenty-six when she met Burt, already consigned to spinster-hood by most of her acquaintances. She was the middle of the three Bereman girls, all of whom were bright, independent, proud, and single. Fay, Jessie's pretty little sister, was frequently courted, but boys were intimidated by her self-sufficient ways and terrified by Theo, her stern oldest sister. Years later, when I asked my father why his aunts had never married, he laughed and said that they never found anyone good enough. Perhaps no man was brave or confident enough to match wits with them. Or maybe they simply preferred their independence.

I try to imagine their meeting, my grandfather and grandmother. Both a bit older than the norm for coupling in those days, both meticulous—she a bookkeeper, he secretary to the auditor of the Pacific Express Company—both handsome and apparently comfortable in society. Burton was active in the world of music and he kept a journal, as had Jessie's father during the War between the States, perhaps marking him in her mind as a man of sensitivity and culture. And he was deeply smitten with Jessie.

Maybe Burt's charm eclipsed Jessie's penchant for freedom. But also I think of the contrast between her office job, allowing almost no contact with children, and the life of her younger sister, a grade-school teacher thoroughly involved in the blossoming of her young students. Perhaps Jessie was beginning to feel an ache to have children of her own. Or maybe she simply fell for the handsome Mr. Searle.

And so it was that on September 6, 1899, Jessie Knox Bereman and Burton Leonard Searle were married. Early the next year they moved to Kirkwood, Missouri, outside of St. Louis. In January of 1902 Leonard Bereman was born, followed in a bit under two years by little Jimmy, who would become my father—James Dorman, named for the Dorman family who had raised Burt after his parents died.

Spurred by its role as railroad hub for western expansion, St. Louis had become the country's fourth-largest city by the late 1880s, booming both economically and culturally. A center for ragtime and jazz music, it was the home of Scott Joplin in the early 1900s. Burt took advantage of the city's cultural opportunities, touring with the choral society that would become the St. Louis Symphony Orchestra. St. Louis was also a founding member of the National Baseball League; their team became the Cardinals in 1900. And how many other cities in those days boasted a Ladies' Cycling Club? In 1904, celebrating the hundredth anniversary of the Louisiana Purchase, St. Louis hosted both the World's Fair and the Summer Olympics. It was a heady time.

Railroads, the Railway Express Agency, and industry provided the fuel for this cultural feast. There were breweries and distilleries, flour mills, slaughterhouses, tobacco processing, lead mining, and paint-, brick-, and iron-manufacturing. As industries grew, real estate, construction, and the economy boomed; offal, spilth, and dregs flowed; smoke and coal dust filled the air; and buildings, trees, and the sky grew dark, smudged with grime. Beginning in the 1890s, efforts to control pollution collided with the desire to promote growth. It would be nearly three decades before progress was made toward cleaner living conditions, and even in the twenty-first century, children in East St. Louis suffer disproportionally from asthma and other respiratory diseases.

Though dirty, St. Louis was also exciting. Driven by visions of unlimited resources and conquest of the West, eager entrepreneurs experienced both giddy successes and inevitable downturns. A stock crash in 1901 was followed by a recession from 1902 to 1904 and again from 1907 to 1911 (except for a small rally in 1909), all accompanied by predictable speculation, buying and selling, winners and losers. A dominant player by the latter quarter of the nineteenth century, early in 1910, Wells Fargo acquired a controlling interest in the Pacific Express Company, where Burton had worked since 1897. Late in the summer of 1911, Wells Fargo bought the company outright. Though I have nothing to go on but guesswork, by late 1911, my grandfather's job must have seemed, at best, a bit insecure.

The Homestead Act of 1862 promised 160 acres to anyone who would build a house, plant a crop, and maintain a residence for five years. By the early 1900s most of the good farming land had been settled. The Act was updated in 1909, 1912, and 1916, decreasing residency requirements to three years and increasing the land allotment to 320 acres, or 640 for people wanting to run cattle. Meanwhile, the Great Northern Railroad Company, hoping to increase its customer base with new settlers, their shipments of household and farm supplies and their envisioned outgoing products, promoted the arid, sagebrush-covered high plains of northern Montana as having a healthful climate, winters that were not severe because of the dry air, and fertile soils from which farmers could expect "phenomenal" yields of winter wheat.

That might have sounded like a godsend to my grandparents. The doctor had recently counseled Burton to find work out of doors in clean air, informing him that his very life depended on getting away from the industrial pollution that hung so heavily over the St. Louis area. I was never privy to the nature of his malady. Though tuberculosis and asthma were rampant, to my knowledge Grandfather had neither. But Burton was an outdoorsman who had for years shared a hunting lodge with some friends. He read of a northern Montana town called Valier, close to Lake Francis—a large water body built for irrigation, primarily by the largesse of a local cattleman—advertising an abundance of water fowl and fishing, with nearby hunting for mule and white tail deer, pheasants and grouse. The Homestead Act, the doctor's pronouncement, and the tenuous job situation, along with the city's pollution and Burton's love of the outdoors, must have been an irresistible combination.

So in the spring of 1912, Jessie and Burt packed up the little boys, then eight and ten, and followed the route blazed by Lewis and Clark—north and west with the Missouri. Between 1909 and 1923, 114,620 adventurous souls settled claims in new territories. My grandparents left behind their green river valley, stimulating social lives, history of urban office jobs, Jessie's family, and Burt's hunting buddies for clean air, a distant view of the Rocky Mountains, isolation, bitter cold, and winds blowing dry soil where little grew. The comparative statistics alone are stunning: Kirkwood, Missouri, sits at an elevation of 660 feet and averages thirty-nine inches of precipitation annually. Valier's elevation is 3,800 feet, with an average of twelve inches of precipitation a year. A seven-year drought began in 1916, some years so severe that wheat would not even sprout. In years that it did grow well, it could be devoured by grasshoppers or destroyed by hail. Of those nearly 115,000 new settlers, many gave up, some just walking away, leaving everything behind, including their cattle.

But not my grandparents. They were determined folks, both of stubborn stock not inclined to admit either defeat or nostalgia. I don't sense that they were happy, though. I imagine Jessie feeling ripped from her family, from culture, from civilization. Though as far as I know neither had background in farming, ranching, or construction (I always wonder how they built *their* house), I believe both worked diligently on the farm. I picture Burt trying to create something he could call good, not voicing frustrations or worries, but withdrawing—seeming solitary and critical—then trying unsuccessfully to interest either of his boys in taking over the farm, while perhaps Jessie quietly encouraged them to expand their horizons. After college, Leonard began teaching agricultural sciences in the local high school; Dorman (no longer "Jimmy" and later still, simply "J. D." to his colleagues) studied law. In the years I knew my grandfather, he reminisced about his boyhood in Vermont, but spoke rarely of the twenty-four years in Montana. Perhaps that was because it was so hard, but maybe it was because of how it ended.

When the boys went away to college, Jessie felt a renewed need for an independent life. Burt was upset when she found a bookkeeping job in the nearby town of Valier. I imagine him fretting, *Do you want people to think I can't support my wife?* But he didn't object when she bought a car with her first year's earnings. He remembered how terrified he and the boys had been when a horse spooked and the team she had been driving from her buggy ran away with her. And through the years he came to accept, if never relish, her employment.

On January 12, 1935, Jessie took the Model A and headed to town in the midst of a snowstorm. The road had been plowed but new snow was coming so fast that looking through the windshield was like looking into a white blanket. A half-hour down the road, the car got stuck in a snow bank. She tried to rock it, tried to push it backward, tried and tried to start it so that she could put it in reverse. She could probably smell gas, and was undoubtedly getting very cold. She might have had the rueful thought that those horses wouldn't have been such a bad bet that day. A neighbor lived nearby but Jessie almost certainly would have rejected asking for help, if the thought even occurred to her. It was only a couple of miles home, walking cross-country. She would be just fine.

Snow drifted over the tops of fences and was thick in the air. She had a sense of the right direction even though no landmarks were visible. The snow was crusty, but not thick enough to hold her weight. She would sink through, each step an effort. Occasionally she could make out a fence post, helping her orient herself. She held the fence once, and lost a glove there. Trying to channel her, I imagine that as she began to get sleepy, it made her cross. *Only the indolent take naps in the daytime.* She willed herself to wake up, to keep walking.

A flurry of thoughts probably chased through her mind. She would have missed her sisters. Theo would be retiring soon. Maybe she would come out to Valier for a visit. Her sons, Leonard and Dorman, were doing well.

They had good wives. Perhaps she smiled, thinking of Dorman's pretty three-year-old Nancy, and wondered if there would be more grandchildren. She was glad Roosevelt had been elected president. He would take care of all those people hurting so badly after '29. She had helped elect him! Little Nancy would never know how it had felt to fight for the right to vote. Jessie staggered, fell, struggled back to her feet, and lifted heavy legs once again into the snow.

They found her the next day on the back edge of the property she and Burt shared. A few items of apparel—a glove, a hat, a scarf—showed that toward the end she had been walking in circles. But she nearly made it.

I know my grandmother through her photos and her beautiful dress, through her sons, her husband, and her sisters. It is solely from those components that I try to form the whole person. I can only guess and imagine who she was, but I know she was an important part of who I am. Clearly some of her DNA resides within me—the stubborn, willful, I-can-take-care-of-myself part. But I believe that the most important thing I gained from her was the respect for women that she taught my father.

6
Considering Economics

It is not the man who has too little, but the
man who craves more that is poor.
—L. A. SENECA

"It's the economy, stupid," Bill Clinton's presidential campaign famously proclaimed. In our society, money management is a criterion for success both for the government and the individual. But David and I have flunked that test more often than we have passed it. One of the earliest economic misadventures on our property happened when we excavated a lovely big pond designed by our nephew, who was at the time an agricultural engineering student at Oregon State University. We hired a contractor we didn't know to do the work, based on the good job his uncle had done constructing our driveway. We had decided just how much we would be able to spend on the job. The contractor agreed and started digging, but because of his inexperience with estimating our sort of project, he was not yet to the halfway point when he reached the designated bottom of our funds, if not of the pond.

So what to do? After fuming, weighing alternatives, calculating, and losing lots of sleep, we decided to sell the rest of Grandfather's stocks, which I had inherited from my father, in order to finish the job. This was in the mid-1980s; the country was in a recession, and the stocks were worth only two-thirds of their former value. Still, we weren't as distressed as we might have been: owning stocks seemed to us an exercise in magical thinking. Why should a piece of paper be worth more or less on a given day just because someone proclaims it to be so? And it hadn't even been our money that went into the purchases of the original pieces of paper. But magic or not, once we made the sale, the golden-egg-laying goose was dead.

Just as our method of financing the pond would never have appeared in the best practices section of anyone's financial plan, May 2008 was an odd time to begin building a house. The nation was in the early stages of the worst downturn since the Great Depression of the 1930s. All around us, the economy was contracting: businesses laying off workers, retirement funds vaporizing, vacations being rerouted to the patio, home-improvement plans being filed in a "Someday Maybe" folder, and banks failing.

We, on the other hand, being self-employed on a part-time basis but officially retired, had no jobs to lose and, perhaps a bit like the folks who store their life savings in their mattresses, we felt our small nest egg would be safest if it hatched into a house. Before we shrank our savings by putting in the septic system and making the required driveway improvements, we had thought that what was left of the money from selling our house in town (after we paid off all of our debts) might be enough to buy the necessary materials for our country house. If we did all of the building ourselves, we possibly could afford to complete it. But acknowledging the pace we work, our rough calculation put the finish date at about . . . sometime in the fall of 2168.

"So," I said, being less impressed with risk-avoidance in the financial realm than the retired are advised to be, "whaddya say we go for broke—literally?"

That's when we called Curtis and decided to see how much we could get done before the money ran out. If all the goddesses of luck were with us, we were hoping to at least get the house up and closed (walls, windows, doors, roof, siding) before winter.

Curtis has been a gift. He works hard and efficiently—no idle chit-chat, no beer breaks. With knowledge built from experience, he works with care and takes pride in his accomplishments. And he doesn't charge an arm and a leg. We are grateful for that, but also feel a bit guilty. We definitely are getting more than our money's worth, whatever that means. I find it impossible to rationalize the great disparity you see in incomes. Why, for instance, should a CEO get four hundred times the hourly pay of the people who do the work? Why should Curtis, who does exemplary work, earn less than contractors who don't come when they say they will, don't return calls, charge for fat-chewing time?

The inequity question came home to me back in my professional gardening days, when my doctor asked if I would like to work off my bill. Having twenty-four hours in a day like everyone else but more limited income than many, I appreciated the suggestion. It wasn't until I was midway through my work in her yard that I realized the lie of "having twenty-four hours like everyone else." If time is money, my day was far shorter. Of course no one would expect to pay the same for a doctor's services as for those of a gardener, yet I had never considered how much less an hour of my life was worth compared to someone else's. But clearly it was, if money was the measure.

Curtis won't become wealthy working more for love than for money, but his life is rich nonetheless. His work itself is rewarding, as the appreciation of his clients must also be. And focusing on the quality of life rather than his bank balance, he re-charges his batteries by camping, climbing, and backpacking.

I admire his priorities, which shows perhaps that I have a very un-American (or at least un-capitalistic) attitude toward money. This may come from my natural contrariness, or perhaps it's an adaptation of my mother's overt derision of conspicuous consumption. To some degree it also likely arose from the social era I was born into. My generation was wedged between the excesses of the twenties and the war fever and post-war boom of the forties. It was a small generation. A mid-western farmer, looking back on that period, observed, "We weren't growing much—crops or children." The nation was in the midst of a deep depression. Jobs and money both were scarce. Who needed the extra pressure of kids to care for?

I can understand how living with little could birth a hunger for security or wealth for its own sake, but what I learned, both by observation and by experience, was to find satisfaction in creating my own entertainment, as well as appreciation for the freedom from striving toward someone else's goal. I still remember the perverse pride in which I showed off the holes in the soles of my shoes my freshman year in college. I could manage just fine, thank you very much (back in the days when state support made college affordable, with a bit of extra effort) with no fat financial jet stream to propel me—and for which I would be beholden.

We were the last pre-electrical-grid generation in the United States. The east coast became electrified bit by bit, starting at about the turn of the twentieth century, but electricity spread west slowly, and more slowly still to rural areas. In early May of 1935, the year of my birth, President Roosevelt, by executive order, created the Rural Electricity Administration as a jobs-opportunity program. In that same year, the Hoover Dam was built. Within two years, one and a half million farms gained power. Living just two miles south of the southwest Washington town of Chehalis, we had electricity from my earliest childhood memories in the late 1930s, but we used little of it. We cooked our meals on a wood-fired range; another woodstove heated the house. I was four or five when we got a refrigerator. Until then we had an ice box (which I don't remember) and kept many things in a cabinet cooler—a cupboard vented to the outside, with screen-covered holes in the wall. We continued using the cooler for butter, eggs, jam, molasses, and syrup, among other items, long after getting the refrigerator.

My father's aunt from St. Louis visited us in the spring of 1941 and was distressed to see my mother heating her iron's removable plates on the stove as she prepared to press clothes for herself and her family of two daughters (with another on the way), a husband, and father-in-law. After Auntie Fay went home, and shortly before my sixth birthday, a lovely lightweight Sunbeam electric iron arrived in the mail from St. Louis. The old irons were heavy and the way the plates clipped on gave numerous avenues for a good burn, so little girls were not allowed the privilege of ironing. But after Auntie Fay's iron arrived, I was thrilled and proud to be allowed to iron my own small handkerchiefs.

Our electricity was adequate for lights, refrigerator, iron, radio, and the wringer washer that plugged into a light socket. Clothes flapped dry on a clothesline or occasionally, in really wet weather, hung on wooden racks in the house. We operated the record player with a hand-crank. But in the early forties when we visited our maternal grandmother, along with various aunts, uncles, and cousins, at the "Stump Ranch," their logged-over spread ten more miles out of town, we did completely without either electricity or indoor plumbing. Lanterns lit the dark; those removable iron plates, or bricks, heated in the oven and wrapped in towels, warmed our feet under the covers at night; Grandmother or an aunt pumped water from the well and carried it to the house in buckets. An outhouse was a short walk from the house. Bushes to "go behind" were closer. At night there was the "thunder" ("thunder the bed if you need it"), called a chamber pot by the adult world.

By 1942, the year the Grand Coulee Dam began producing power, half of the nation was wired, if not the Stump Ranch. By the 1950s—the decade in which I finished high school and college, got married, and started a family—most of the United States was electrified. But even today, two billion people on earth live very much as my rural relatives did when we visited them in the 1940s—and as David and I have for eighteen recent years.

These years—nearly two decades now—haven't been a stretch or a big adjustment for us, and we definitely don't see them as a hardship. We have been able to pick and choose. We can remember the simple ways we learned in childhood. We don't seek material accumulation, knowing well that we can't buy happiness. We find entertainment in conversation, reading, writing, and the radio; rewards in the work of growing and preserving our own produce; and thrill in the constant surprises and changes of the natural world, all the while appreciating being able to text or talk to our kids by cell phone or get access to the Internet with a quick trip to the library. It may not be what Bill Clinton had in mind, but our economy suits us very well.

7
A Mentor

To find yourself, think for yourself.
—SOCRATES

Daddy doubtless was attracted to my mother at least partly because of her saucy, independent intelligence. Always appreciative of her capabilities, he nevertheless felt both the responsibility and the appropriateness of being the breadwinner—taking care of his family. But when Mother was crippled with rheumatoid arthritis and osteoporosis in the last decade of her life, he wondered aloud to me if she mightn't have been healthier if she'd channeled her talents into a career.

Daddy expected my sisters and me to use our minds in an age when many females were steered into the fine arts of throwing parties, polishing the silver, husband hunting, and changing diapers. Though my own inclinations, or watching my mother, might have caused me to rebel even if he *had* reflected the sexist mores of the day, I give considerable credit to the effect his attitude had on me. I remember how I trailed his paths, hung on his words.

Daddy was up before light to split and carry wood, getting the fire crackling long before most of the rest of us were willing to give up on our dreams. Some mornings I'd wake early and tag along after him, trying to pile sticks in the crook of my arm like he did, to fill the wood box by the big cast-iron cooking range. Lines like the rays of the sun sprouted from the corners of his gray-blue eyes, and his grin wrinkles spread when he looked down at me in that delighted, full-of-love way I can still see and feel today. Much of Mother's work was relatively stationary—baking, sewing, ironing, doing the wash—and "stationary" was a foreign concept to my little body. So the occasional spoon or beater to lick, or newly designed dress to try on, didn't hold my interest for long. But when Daddy was working outside, I shadowed as closely behind as I could.

He seemed to me to be in perpetual motion. At home, in his blue work shirt, blue jeans, leather work boots, and brimmed felt hat, he worked outside from before sunup until breakfast, cutting bloomed-out rose blossoms, disbudding, fertilizing. Then he fixed our breakfast (hot cereal alternating with eggs and bacon or sausage six days a week, and pancakes on Sunday), a habit he adopted early in marriage when Mother would faint if she got up without first having a glass of orange juice (attributable, I believe, to her having low blood sugar). So first he brought her juice in bed and soon began fixing the whole meal. On weekdays he would change after breakfast into a white shirt and tie, a suit, and shiny black shoes to go to his law office, and the brimmed hat for town had no signs of garden mottling on it. But as soon as he got home, and all day Saturday and Sunday afternoon, he donned his work clothes and headed outside.

Sometimes he would take time from mowing or pruning to play ball with me or let me "help" him. In one of my warm memories he stopped working (I don't remember pestering him, but I probably did) and lay down on the lawn under the apple trees, with me right beside him. We just lay there, watching the shapes and the motion of the clouds. He loved the warm summer days and the luxuriant flowers, fruit, and foliage of the Pacific Northwest, with trees that were green even in the winter—all so different from the landscape of Montana's barren high desert and winter cold that he had known in his growing years. He told me, as we watched cloud patterns, that my mother had taught him how to look at and appreciate the natural world. As I recall him lying there drifting with the clouds, or gazing with delight on the dew-tipped bud of a favorite rose, I think he must have been a pretty good student.

Daddy had a yen to explore the mountains and old-growth forests that surrounded our valley, but rarely felt comfortable breaking away from the office long enough to do much of it. "That might be the moment my million-dollar case comes in," he would joke. But I had my first and only fishing trip during one rare family vacation at Packwood Lake, nearly three thousand feet up in the northern Cascade Mountains of western Washington. I remember Mother oven-drying green beans in preparation for our backpack trip. My next mental picture is of my hyper self, scooting around everyone to be first in line as we hiked, then scooting back again to check on Mother, who stopped to rest now and then. I was probably about ten, so she would have been forty, but she said that her knees were a good thirty years older than that, and they needed to take it easy. When we arrived at the lake, we moved into a lovely little cabin. Log, perhaps. That's the image I have in my head. And that's how I slept—like a log.

As he usually did, Daddy got up in the pre-dawn gray. I tumbled out of bed, eager to be part of whatever enterprise he had in mind. We rowed out on the lake and before long had decked five black-spotted, green and gold rainbow trout with bright pink side-stripes. I recall little of catching them, or what I saw on the lake, but remember well the warmth of the adventure together, the out-of-this-world delicious flavor of those fresh-caught rainbows, and the pride in being back in the cabin with breakfast in hand just as my mother and sisters were waking up.

Beyond the things I did with him, I was tremendously influenced by some of our discussions. Once when I was around ten, I told Daddy that if I was lost or needed help, I could always trust the police, couldn't I?

"Well, probably," he said, looking a bit uncomfortable, "but police are human. There are good ones and bad ones. You should remember that."

And I did; he helped me take a much clearer-eyed look through titles, professions, and uniforms to the fallible humans inside. I got the feeling Daddy was speaking from his own disillusionment, his pain at reaching pragmatism through the idealist's door. Though he never illustrated with personal stories, I felt his vulnerability when he cautioned, "Don't put people on a pedestal. When you discover their clay feet, you'll be disappointed."

We attended the Presbyterian church when I was growing up, not because our parents were Presbyterians (raised Methodist, Daddy was agnostic and Mother, though influenced by Baptist roots, worshiped in her garden) but because they felt "do unto others as you would have them do unto you" and "love your neighbor as yourself" made a healthy social foundation for a child. Maybe Presbyterian was a compromise. Maybe they liked the minister. Or maybe the pretty little church just struck their fancy. On the way home from church we had long analytical discussions about the sermon, considering what made sense and why, and what needed further investigation. Daddy was a card-carrying skeptic and helped us to question whatever we heard or read.

And he taught us to trust our judgment. When I was in junior high, I befriended a boy who was a trustee at the local "training school" (reformatory), and as such, was allowed to attend public school. One evening during halftime at a football game, I walked across the field with him—right there in public! A friend's parent took me aside and scolded me for "risking ruining (my) father's reputation." I was alarmed at the idea and talked with Daddy at the first opportunity.

"My reputation isn't worth much if a little thing like that could ruin it," he reassured me. And he went on to counsel me to make decisions by weighing what was right for me, not worrying about him or the gossips. Later, with my parents' support, I invited the young man home for dinner.

Another lesson took only a few of his well-chosen words. I asked him what he thought of someone's potential mate–the sweetie or perhaps betrothed of a friend or relative. He smiled and said, "It doesn't matter what I think. I'm not the one who has to live with him."

So simple. No "don't gossip" or "don't be judgmental" or "mind your own business," but a clear and reasoned message that stuck tight in my conscience.

Contrary to his good advice, I'm afraid I did put my *father*, at least, on a bit of a pedestal. But rather than finding feet of clay, I discovered a person of flesh and bones who was all too mortal. As his father had lived to be ninety-six, Daddy likely assumed he would be long-lived as well. A sinewy five feet, eight inches tall, at age seventy he out-wrestled his teenage grandson (though it's just possible the teenager pulled his punches a bit), and he was still taking care of the roses, climbing trees, and mowing a couple acres of meadow into his mid seventies. But when he was seventy-five, the oncologist diagnosed advanced bone cancer—giving a prognosis of two years maximum. It was a shock. "I thought I'd at least be able to see Amy through," he said, speaking of my mother, who had been crippled for many years. But when I asked him if he was worried about her, he said, "No. It doesn't do any good to worry."

He had always been proud of his fitness and had felt that at death he would want his body to remain intact. But now it had let him down, so when the time came, he figured we might as well have it cremated. He rejected any extreme treatments that would only prolong his illness and make him feel lousy to boot. He kept working in the yard, going to the office, fixing

Mother's meals, and feeding her when she couldn't get the food from the plate to her mouth.

In the fall he planted an apricot tree because Mother really liked apricots. On Thanksgiving, our daughter Erika brought Gabrielle and Cecilia, friends from Sweden who she had met in college, to spend the holiday with her grandparents, and we all played in two-foot-deep snow, our little dog Arnold disappearing beneath it with each leap, gathering himself up and reappearing only to disappear once more. My father watched from the window with a smile, taking pleasure in our pleasure, though he shook his head, incredulous that anyone could find fun in that much cold. Beth and her husband, Clyde, came as well, along with their four: Kim, Lois, Bill, and Tom, ranging in age from eleven to nearly seventeen. At dinner Daddy wanted to enjoy his food but he couldn't convince his digestive system. Gabrielle had brought Swedish chocolate, and Daddy, the original chocoholic, wanted to want it. If there was doubt in anyone's mind that he was sick, that doubt was extinguished when he couldn't manage even a bite. Kids and grandkids came home again at Christmas and he visited and joked almost like usual, though he was visibly weak. I remember a general milling about among Christmas decorations, but I'm not even sure how many of us were there: my attention was focused on my father. After a short holiday, he went back to work. Then one day he went directly from the office to the hospital. In a week or so, we brought him home. On January 12, 1981, in the quiet, unassuming way that through all of his life he had completed the job set before him, Daddy died.

He never did like the winter.

8

Resourcefulness and Sagacity

*Wisdom exalted her children, and layeth hold of them
that seek her. (S)He that loveth her, loveth life.*

—THE APOCRYPHA

By late September, nights are becoming cooler, the leaf painter once again has splashed scarlet on the poison oak leaves, and our foundation is finished. We say good-bye to Julia and Brad, and Curtis introduces us, one or two at a time, to an assortment of talented and diligent helpers: Eric, Paul, Abel, Rob, Chris, Stewart, Kyle. Our goal is to get a roof on before the rains commence, and yet, the official rain year starts October 1—days away—and we have barely begun the framing.

I had dreamed of working beside David, learning how to saw and nail, actually helping to build our house. But I am the gal who, on my college entrance exams, scored in the top three percentile in language arts, and the *bottom* three percentile—really!—in mechanical aptitude. Clearly, I would need tutoring. Still, it's something I always wanted to learn, from high school days when my friend Barbara and I begged to get into shop class and were gently told that we lacked the muscle. Which really meant we lacked the testosterone: no girls were allowed in shop. Now it is my house, not a class, and I long to help it take shape. Yet as I watch the steady, quiet progress of folks who already know what to do, I see only two choices: be a student or stay out of the way and let the crew work rather than teach. I regretfully put away my student fantasy in favor of the possibility of winter shelter. For my dream to have come true, we would have to have built a cabin.

Even so, I love watching these guys work. First they close in the foundation, laying 4x6 fir girders parallel to span from the north to the south walls and setting joists on sixteen-inch centers perpendicularly above the girders.

Then they begin gluing and nailing down three-quarter-inch tongue-and-groove plywood sub-flooring. This creates a platform—a site for a dance, perhaps, or a forum. Before long I can see the metamorphosis to "house" begin. The sub-flooring serves as a table where the crew assembles the walls. They nail the studs into their appropriate positions, frame holes for doors and windows, then tilt up a completely framed wall.

Once I acknowledge that I'm not going to get in on the actual building, I go back to work on what I've been neglecting during these weeks of the gestation and birth of the house: taking care of our nursery plants and working in the vegetable garden. We grow the plants at the lowest elevation of our very hilly property. Thirty or so feet higher, beside the pond, is our campsite, the pond being enough higher than the garden and nursery that we can gravity-feed water from it for irrigation. I keep sufficiently busy—repotting plants, weeding, watering, planting salad greens for fall and garlic for next summer—that I miss ongoing changes in the house. But it's comforting to hear the steady *Bang! Bang!* of the nail guns. Every few days as I walk up from our tent or back down to work in the garden, another bit of the stick house appears, and I gasp to see Curtis scrambling monkey-like along 2x4s high in the air, climbing on the joists that will eventually support our upper-level flooring. Neither David nor I are particularly agile or even very steady on narrow high places, so once again, we see the wisdom of getting help.

Asking for help is not any more natural for me than it was for Jessie, that grandmother of mine who froze to death trying to find her way home, though a neighbor lived near where the snowbank swallowed her car. I grew up feeling that I should make my own way in the world and solve my own problems. But David and I are now both nearly three years beyond our biblically allotted lifespan of three-score and ten. If we were committed to build the house ourselves, we would take how long? Fifteen years maybe? Twenty? When my mother used to say, "Make the best of it," what I heard was "Don't complain." But after several decades, I heard the actual words: "Make the *best* of it." I need to look beyond my preconceptions to understand a situation as it exists. Having been dealt this particular hand (in my case, never having learned the art of carpentry—plus the fact that neither of us is getting any younger), how should I play it for the best possible results? Trying to play it as do-it-yourself homebuilders is just practicing make-believe. And the fact of its being make-believe might have contributed to our daughter's early concerns about us.

Erika, our firstborn, was innately long on empathy. As a small child, she wept one evening when her little brother, Jeff, went to bed without brushing his teeth. So convinced was she of the necessity of dental care, she was terrified that his teeth would rot and all fall out before morning. Through the years she counseled neighbor children, anticipated the needs of guests, sought out aged relatives who were sitting alone at family gatherings, and at age twelve, presented me with an elegant Mother's Day breakfast on the deck. It shouldn't have been a surprise, then, that she was concerned when her parents moved to the woods and a simple life just a few years short of retirement age. When I tried to argue that we were fine, she asked how I would have felt if it had been *my* parents there. That stopped me—not because I would have worried about them, but because I couldn't imagine it. Daddy's strong sense of responsibility as provider was such that it just wouldn't have happened. But I *could* imagine my ingenious, nature-loving mother enjoying the challenge, should it have presented itself.

Mother was adventurous and creative. Having grown up with little, and then raising her own children during the Depression, she was the master of "make do." She seemed to delight in finding a new solution to old problems. She could mend most anything, but if it couldn't be fixed or re-used, she would make use or ornament of the remnants. She made a big ball from the string in the tops of flour and sugar bags, always handy when we needed to tie something, and she made us dresses out of the bags. She darned socks; patched everything—including the sheets; turned collars as the neck-side began to fray; remodeled Daddy's old suits to make fashionable outfits for her girls; grew, baked, and preserved food for her family's meals; and I remember a springy doormat, made from canning-jar rubbers. She was the epitome of Kipling's "infinite resourcefulness and sagacity."

Mother was also a noticer. She helped her family see the little things—the dew drops on spider webs, the hump and stretch of an inchworm, the golden whorl of stamens in the center of a rose. I think she would have delighted in our woodland paradise and I know she would have managed quite well without modern conveniences.

Along with her attention to and pleasure in nature and her creative skill-fulness and wisdom, she had a furious independence. She could not only manage and improvise, she would do it her own way and without help. She was just a teenager when women won the right to vote, but I can imagine her pleasure, and how she might have uttered, with a toss of the head and hands on hips, "Well, it's about time!"

She was all of twenty when she and her big brother Foy bought a Model-T Ford, the first auto in the family. They pooled their resources—hers, I believe, mostly from working on ranches, feeding the farm hands. I see my mother when I think of Amelia Earhart, who was just seven years Mother's senior. Mother was a feminist before there were feminists, a hippie before there were hippies. Watching her, I never had reason to believe my gender or the proscriptions of others should narrow my horizons.

Through the years I was often in awe of my mother, but sometimes she shocked me. "We were good to our slaves," she once told me. My jaw dropped. We had *slaves? We* had slaves? *Good* to them? Yeah, sure! And they pass out candy and milkshakes in the gulag.

I was in my mid teens, and very sure about right and wrong, good and bad. I and mine were supposed to be in the white-hat column; but having slaves was inarguably wrong and bad. Mother watched me closely, her face looking as if it might break, so I didn't voice the chaos inside of me. I did ask what being good to them meant, thinking sarcastically, "not beating them very hard?"

"We taught them to read and write," Mother said, "and treated them like family." I mumbled something and left the room, feeling sick to my stomach and thinking, "Big deal. Everybody learns how to read and write. Big bloody deal. *You had slaves!*"

Years and a bit of education later, I discovered that indeed it was a very big deal. Far, far from everybody learns to read and write, and educating your slaves may have been a capital offense. Rather than just "being good," the owners were being principled and courageous. I wish I'd not been so damned know-it-all-judgmental and had asked a question or two. Maybe I'd have actually learned something. Of course Mother herself might have had few details. "We" was a word taking responsibility for genetic history. Emancipation came, after all, not only forty-three years before *she* was born, but eighteen years before the birth of her *mother*. She, like I, knew only what she had been told.

What she was told as a child in Virginia was doubtless far different from what my southwest Washington ears were tuned to hear in the late 1940s and early 1950s. I knew we had family in gray uniforms as well as blue during the Civil War. And I heard the lingering sorrow and bitterness when Mother told of Sherman's fiery destruction through Georgia and the Carolinas, the heart of the Confederacy. But mostly her Virginia memories were sweet: hoecake and buttermilk, spinach with bacon grease, fresh bread with syrup, nostalgic Southern songs. We learned, "Down by the canebrake close beside the sea / lived a little colored gal her name was Nancy Lee / told her that I loved her, loved her very long / goin' to serenade her and this'll be my song: Come my love, my boat lies low / she rides high and dry on the O-hi-o / Come my love, oh come along with me / and I'll take you down to Tennessee."

I never heard even a hint of racism. When I was growing up Mother taught the three-year-olds at Sunday School. Those little ones, along with Mother's three girls, were raised on another song, "Black and yellow, red and white / they are precious in his sight / Jesus loves the little children of the world." And nothing throughout school gave me any reason to doubt that accepted core of equality.

So I felt quite confident when I recounted to my parents a discussion I'd had in my first year of college: Some of us Caucasian teenagers were asked how our families would react if we were to find Black partners. I assured the group that there would be no problem at my house. "My parents would care what sort of person he was inside, not the color of his skin." As I sat across from Mother and Daddy, a big empty white space filled the void between us. Not a sound. My parents just looked at each other until finally Mother swallowed and said, "I *hope* that's the way we would feel."

This time, though again shocked, I wasn't appalled. I was proud of them for raising us with no tinge of bias when it was apparent they had traveled a long rough road themselves. Whatever the social attitudes that had shaped them, they were able to open their minds and hearts to find new ways. And they chose not to infect their daughters with residual germs of prejudice.

There were innumerable other things my mother taught me. She would send us out to run naked in warm rain when we were little girls, teaching us life is to be enjoyed and bodies are not shameful.

She had great disdain for popular parenting in which a trespassing little one was dragged by the ear to "say you're sorry." She felt forced apologies taught that words were more important than deeds—taught dishonesty and superficiality.

She taught us to respect not only our words and deeds, but also our emotions. When I was a jilted and broken-hearted fifteen-year-old, trying to be adult, I smiled through my sobs and said, with not a little drama, "Someday I'll look back on this and laugh." Mother looked squarely at me and said, "I hope not." Just those three words validated my feelings and myself.

My parents' relationship with each other also made a deep impression on me. They would hold hands when they strolled the garden together and frequently end up in each other's arms in front of the stove as we dawdled at the table. We girls would complain—"Aww, mush!"—but we loved it.

With Mother in the lead, we would all kiss Daddy good-bye when he left for work and eagerly greet him with hugs and kisses on his return in the evening. They talked, sometimes quietly and confidentially, sometimes where we could join in; they laughed and teased; but—at least in our hearing—never argued.

My strongest memory of Mother from childhood is of her busyness. I remember the hours she spent cooking: baking bread, pies, rolls, cookies, and canning fruit and vegetables, grape juice, mincemeat, applesauce, and jam. Each Monday she washed clothes in the old wringer washer, hung them on the line, rushed them in to avoid a shower. On Tuesdays she ironed the whole pile, which was to be folded *just so*, keeping Daddy's shirts looking professionally pressed, and linens fitting perfectly in assigned spaces on their shelves.

The clothes, along with everything else, she put in precise locations in drawers and shelves. She knew where everything was, and it all fit tidily because of the way she had folded it. Her garden also was as immaculate as it was beautiful, and her life was carefully scheduled. There was a time to get up, a time to start dinner, a time for her children and herself to go to bed. She always got to appointments early. She requested "thirty minutes written notice" to stop or turn when she was driving (a joke, but heartfelt, nonetheless). She didn't like surprises, tickling, lavender, Bartok, ripe olives, or facial hair on men.

Mother was a quoter. She had a prodigious memory and would recite endlessly from Tennyson, Shakespeare, Whitman, Kipling, the Bible. So many lessons. *"And this above all: to thine own self be true, and it must follow, as the night the day, thou canst not then be false to any man."* I rarely knew when the wisdom I was hearing originated with Mother or was from her boundless memory bank, but it all rang true.

I learned from her example and from her advice, and also from things I would like to have been different. In her later years Mother was horribly crippled from rheumatoid arthritis and osteoporosis. Rather than stabilizing, which apparently was the norm, she kept deteriorating, so doctors found her case particularly "interesting," and she became something of a guinea pig. Watching the effects of numerous drugs made me determined to stick with methods that would bolster my body's own defenses. I gained little trust in the great world of the pharmacopeia.

All of my young life Mother had been strong, stubborn, and independent. In later life she remained stubborn, but her strength and independence could be expressed only in her will, not in physical things—in her being, rather than her doing. She had been a popular lecturer on gardening and flower arranging, but she couldn't bear to be seen as less capable, needing someone to maneuver her wheelchair, needing help of almost any kind. Besides not wanting to seem—or be—in any way needy, she shuddered at her very appearance. She had always carried herself regally and would drill her daughters in good posture.

"Tummies in; back straight; tuck in your bottom; head high; long neck; chin in. Everything dangles from an imaginary string at the back of your head. Relax your knees. Now smile!"

Perhaps in her mind still the glamorous flapper, she couldn't abide her gnarled, twisted body, much less let others see it. So she not only chose to stop giving her lectures, she no longer went out in public at all. It seemed to me that her beautiful garden, which had been a constant pleasure and therapy through the years, was no longer a source of joy. As Daddy drove her around the property in their little golf cart, what she seemed to see instead of the beauty were weeds, plants needing to be moved, flaws she was no longer able to fix. The deep satisfaction the garden had always given her was in the work, and then in seeing the results. Daddy continued to work in the garden, but it was Mother who had always been the weeder, the tidier, the choreographer. (*This red should be moved over to that purple section. These lacy gray leaves would look better with the bold dark ones across the garden.*) They hired help, but as any dedicated gardener knows, no one else can do it like you can do it yourself. Now that she couldn't do any of the work, what she saw in the garden was what needed to be done.

But she still did delight in the scenes through the window: the iridescent bronze and green rufous hummingbird sipping nectar from a honeysuckle; the black-winged, butter-yellow goldfinch picking seeds from the bloomed-out aster heads; dots of pink, yellow, red and white that were blossoms in the distant rose beds. And always, always she delighted in her family—her grandchildren, her children, her husband.

After Daddy died, the Presbyterian minister came to the house to discuss the memorial service. Though Mother didn't voice it, her face showed reluctance bordering on dread at the prospect of meeting with him. The minister—the service—only made the unacceptable more real. As we wheeled her to the living room, she gasped, and cried out as if in sudden pain.

"What is it, Mother?" I asked.

"My heart," she said, her hand on her chest.

"It hurts?"

"It's broken."

Once her beloved husband was gone, Mother didn't know what she had to live for. "There's you girls," she said, "but you have your own lives."

So being the sort of take-charge person she was, she went about dying: she refused food. She once told me that if she couldn't feed herself, she didn't deserve to eat. The "deserve" part rankled me, but her decision provided yet another lesson. I know now that when living is no longer fun, I needn't keep at it.

On February 20, thirty-nine days after my father's death, I drove the hundred and eighty miles from Eugene to Chehalis, leaving home after dinner. I tiptoed in around midnight to find Mother thoroughly awake, anticipating my arrival. The night nurse in bed across the room nodded but then turned to go back to sleep.

Mother and I had a short happy visit, but I felt guilty keeping her up at that hour. "You need your sleep," I said, giving her a kiss and turning to go upstairs.

"See you in the morning," she said.

Early the next morning, the nurse came upstairs to wake me. "You need to come."

When I saw Mother lying there still, so still, I thought, *No! You can't be dead!*

The little girl inside of me rubbed her fists in her eyes, snuffling. *You promised! You said you'd see me in the morning! You've never ever broken a promise to me. Never!*

I stood and stared. Little girl. Big girl. Middle-aged orphan woman.

The nurse startled me from my daze, "She was so looking forward to your visit," she said.

Looking around, I caught sight of Mother's wheelchair and a great fireball swelled inside of me. I was consumed with fury. I wanted to kick the chair across the room and through the plate glass window. I guess at some level I blamed the wheelchair for her needing it—saw it as something that *took* her independence, rather than something that had the ability to increase it. Or maybe I just needed to blame something—anything—for the sorrow and loss I felt, not only from my mother's death, but so sharply, for having gone to *bed*, damnit, for not having been with my mother when she died.

Mother was more clever than I by half. She didn't give me her exceptional memory or her talents. But she did give me immense gifts: resilience, curiosity, a can-do attitude, and perhaps, though I don't recall her ever doing it herself, the common sense to know when it's best to ask for help.

9
Still Considering Economics

To cherish what remains of the Earth and foster its
renewal is our only legitimate hope of survival.
—WENDELL BERRY

The World War II generation went before David's and mine; Vietnam, civil rights, sex, drugs, and rock and roll were the hallmarks of the generation after. I marched in war protests with our kids in tow, and got teargassed once—fortunately on a day I'd left them home. Had I not been a parent, I would have headed for the South to join the fight for civil rights. I anguished at what was happening there, as I stayed home, safe and impotent. With a foot in each decade, my generation was out of step with either, but I picked up attitudes from both.

I admired my mother's ability to make something from almost nothing, to feed and clothe her family well, spending time and ingenuity but little cash. Looking back at it, I'm especially impressed that she seemed to maintain an upbeat, curious, attentive perspective even when a stressful economy and the fears and loss of war could understandably push a person to far darker states. Her attitude undoubtedly helped me to realize that the road to happiness lies more in outlook than income, more in how you think than in what you have. And now I believe that the aura of contentedness she conveyed came as well from the work itself—from her creative and successful solutions to challenges.

When I decided in my dotage that I wanted to live more harmoniously with the world, I was met with contradictions and conundrums. I knew several people who had chosen to live the simple life *after* having made a fortune through business or luck. With those funds they easily could invest in all of the current "greenest," most sustainable gadgets and technologies. But it seemed to me we should be able to be at least as "green" as my parents were, without being wealthy. Years ago I was moved by a man I met at a WAND (Women's Action for New Directions) meeting. When he had heard that half of the world's population lived on two dollars a day or less, he vowed that he would do the same, and spent the rest of his life doing just that. I was inspired: *I want to do that too*! I didn't take on the challenge, though, but the goal of simple living never left my mind. Still, I see the incongruity of wanting to make a small footprint while living as far out as we do, where we must drive more frequently and more miles than I would prefer. I rationalize my choice knowing that it is necessary to have our natural places maintained, but then I feel guilty I'm not doing a better job of the maintenance—specifically, failing to eliminate invasive plants.

But in fact, there is great benefit in simply preserving a bit of wildness. Currently forestland runs from Coyote Creek south and east of us, along the south portion of our and our neighbors' properties, uphill to private forest, and then to BLM land. If we, and each of our neighbors, keep a large portion of that wooded, we can maintain a wildlife corridor, assuming Territorial Highway and the fence alongside allow critter through-traffic.

Although Oregon's Forest Practices Act requires re-planting after harvesting timber, a newly planted monoculture has almost nothing ecologically in common with an established mixed-species woodland. When aboveground ecosystem structure changes, so it does belowground. And when structure changes, so does function. A forest is composed of myriad interdependent organisms—the trees, their understory, fungi, fungi-dependent microorganisms, arthropods, amphibians, birds, mammals, and more. Masses of fungal threads permeate most soils—more than eight miles of cells in a cubic inch of healthy soil. This interconnected mycelial mantle recycles carbon, nitrogen, sulfur, iron, and other essential nutrients. Roots of most plants join with specialist fungal threads (mycorrhizae), thus increasing by up to one hundred times the zone where plant roots can find water and nutrients. Researchers have recently shown that mycorrhizae even help plants communicate. A plant being attacked by insects changes its chemistry to repel the onslaught, as it sends out other chemical signals to attract predator insects to prey on the attacker. Scientists have known that other plants pick up such signals through the air, but only recently found that communications also travel through the soil, by way of mutual mycorrhizal connections.

At the same time, the plants feed their fungal partners sugars that they have photosynthesized. Each species is dependent on the other, species that can be destroyed if forests are cut or sprayed, or land is developed. And we humans are dependent on nature's services.

I prefer the term "services" to "resources," but better yet, "gifts." Resources imply they are there for us to use—including, perhaps, to use up. A service needs to be cared for to be maintained. On the other hand, "service" might indicate that its raison d'être is to serve humanity rather than our being most fortunate recipients. "Takers," some would say.

Although any of us living in wood houses appreciate that lumber comes from forests, we less often appreciate forests as the main source of water. A forest receives, stores, purifies, and gradually releases water into streams both above and belowground. As glaciers and snow packs melt, a forest as water source is ever more critical.

Forests also provide habitat for pollinators (insects, birds, bats) and for those that prey on the insects that prey on our crops or make us sick. Many forest fungi, plants, and animals, in addition to their critical interdependent roles, can be used by humans for food and medicine. Forest soils interwoven with thousand of fungal species capture and hold moisture as well as carbon, making them critical players in moderating excess carbon dioxide in the atmosphere.

My friend Chantal, a French national who works for some nursery friends of ours, suggests that every American group debating the use of our natural systems should include at least one European to remind the locals of what they have. When Chantal came to this country, she found our Pacific Northwest almost terrifying. She could hardly believe her eyes as she discovered the giant trees, the thick forest cover, the myriad wild animals and birds. "I'd never seen such things," she said. "But before I came here, I didn't know what I was missing." Initially she reacted very like the early pioneers—overwhelmed, even frightened. To many of the pioneers, though, the response was to tame the wilderness. Subdue it. Like breaking a horse, show it who is boss.

Not so for Chantal. Soon her fear changed to love. After she began to know and understand our wild places, she came to realize what much of Europe had lost. There is a reason, after all, that the marble structures of Greek temples are carved to look like wood. That's what the original ones were made of until the forests were all gone. Chantal says American environmental groups need a European to tell them, "We took it for granted, and now it's gone. Europe is almost all tame. You still have some wilderness. Cherish it!"

Europe has lost nearly half of its former mycorrhizal fungal species. As fungi diminish, disease blooms. Diversity of animals, from insects to mammals, decreases; humidity drops; bare soils blow away; deserts encroach and the climate becomes more extreme. I hope it doesn't take losing our wild places for us to appreciate them, but maybe if we understand that what we have *can* be lost, we'll work harder to preserve it.

So though it's true that I live here because I want to, I like to think that the biosphere might suffer a bit less from this little spot we're keeping wild, even if we do continue to drive. And my guilt over non-maintenance is just one more example of inflating my own importance. I do want to knock back the invasives and to complement the communities by adding appropriate plants, but a sufficiently diverse ecosystem will take care of itself as it works toward balance. If it is dependent on me, as with a neglected garden or a ramshackle house, once I am gone, it will be gone as well.

I greatly admire "eco-cities"—urban areas where people can easily walk to the places they need to go, compact mixes of commerce, residences, professional offices, art studios, educational institutions, and parkland. It's a beautiful, responsible vision, but usually an expensive one. I can utter a mea culpa about living a driving distance from town if I feel the need, but it's a fact that I could never afford to live in one of those lovely green apartments or condominiums. And that's fine, because I'd rather live in the woods anyway, and I need to prove to myself that green living isn't reserved for the well-to-do.

Our society has an odd attitude about money. It's on the list, along with religion and sex, that the Manners Police advise us not to discuss in public. *That's classism! Heaven forfend!* But also unexamined is the fact that in our country, success is implicitly measured in wealth.

A friend once asked me to visit her investment group to talk about my book, *To the Woods*. I worried about it, wondering what I could offer people who were focusing on investments, other than a horrible example. But it occurred to me that in spite of my questionable economic decisions, our goals were really not so different. The women in her group weren't hoping their investments would allow them to line their caskets with bank notes. They were thinking of their families; they were looking for security; they were hoping to finance their hearts' desires. And that's exactly what I wanted as well.

The state of the economy is sometimes measured by consumer satisfaction—and I fight back. I am a *person* (a corporation is not) and a *citizen*. I am *not* a consumer. But of course, I am. It is only in the photosynthetic world that the producers live: the green plants, the algae, the cyanobacteria. We humans, like the rest of the animal world, can't make our own food. We can grow it, preserve it, bake it, but we can't make it. Nor do we make anything else truly from scratch. We are consumers of the gifts of the universe, be they our food, water, air, or minerals. So our choice is not whether, but what, how, and how much we consume. Do we take only what we know will be replaced, thinking always of the seventh generation? Or do we surround ourselves with things in a desperate need to have enough, hoarding perhaps for Y2K or the invasions of aliens or black helicopters or the end of the Mayan calendar?

Humans are not alone in collecting beyond their need. I discovered a great example of that, on a visit to our storage shed. In the back corner, above a stack of large fiber pots, a helter-skelter pile of broken blackberry stems and other sticks nearly reached the roof. I recognized this as a wood rat nest from a description my sister Beth had given me of a huge stick nest built under the hood of her Ford pickup engine. Wood rats make complex dens, with several nest chambers, a food cache area, and debris piles. As I dismantled it, I found a much greater variety of materials than I had expected. Orange, blue, and white pot labels lay about, ready for sign-making maybe: I could imagine "Nursery" or "Pantry" or "No Dogs Allowed." Shreds of newspaper, colored as well as black and white, doubtless made good insulation and added a festive air. Bright golden string zigzagged across the front, looking like an attempt to keep out the riff-raff. A wood rat's version of a gated community, perhaps. Strewn over the top were broken pieces of garlic stems, undoubtedly to ward off the invasion of wood-rat vampires. A worn-out pair of rain pants lay in the midst of it all. Chew out the bottom, stretch it just so, and the little creatures would be well protected if the roof began to leak. Clever fellows, wood rats.

Some of the most interesting collectors I've read about are the bowerbirds of New Guinea and Australia. In preparation for breeding season, the males build elaborate structures that they decorate with sticks and bright objects to attract females. Some bowers are made like maypoles, and others are avenues, with two walls of sticks decorated with such things as shells, leaves, flowers, feathers, stones, berries, coins, rifle shells, plastic or glass pieces, or even spoons or jewelry. Any or all of the precious items might be stolen from nearby campsites, or from a neighbor bird's bower.

Female birds visit several bowers, inspecting the quality. Several females might choose the same bower, to the delight, I imagine, of the successful polygamous male, leaving less-experienced males forlorn. Perhaps the instinct resonates through species. If we pack our nest full maybe we'll attract the best mate. Or we'll have enough for hard times. Or maybe we'll just feel better about ourselves. If the nest gets too full, we can buy another in the Bahamas.

But rather than emulating bower birds or wood rats, (although with my piles of papers, you might wonder) David and I hope to explore the economic questions of life with a more literal definition of *economy*, from the Greek *ecos*, for home, and *nomy*, to manage. We want to manage our home in the most sustainable way. This has nothing to do, really, with the bottom line or consumer satisfaction or the gross national product. What it does entail is learning how to give back as much as we take from the earth. In our *ecos* we want to learn how to be a healthy and functioning strand in the network of the natural system. This is our goal in the construction of a better nest. Let our 401K be a full pantry, our energy a gift from the sun, our medical insurance be fit bodies, our lives ever attuned to our connections to each other and to the lives of each fellow organism on this planet.

10
Stella Barnard Yeatts and Charles Thomas Yeatts

The light that cometh from her wisdom never goeth out.
——THE APOCRYPHA

My mother's mother died at age eighty-eight in a mental institution. The last time I visited her in the state hospital in Warm Springs, Montana, I had trouble finding my grandmother in the woman across the table. Her eyes were dull as she stared into space. She shoved away the salt and pepper, shuddering her head and looking furtively over her shoulder. "I would never use these. They put poison in them, you know. They try to trick you." She was seventy-two then. I was seventeen.

The grandmother I knew had stars in her eyes and red-gold sun in the auburn curls framing her face. She hung out clothes, pumped water from the well, and fed the geese and chickens, all with a laugh and a light step as I trotted behind, trying to help.

She loved to explore. Once as we walked along a path in the meadow, she stopped at a shrub, broke off a twig, and mashed its end to show me how its exposed fibers could make an improvised toothbrush. On another walk we paused in the woods to rest on cushions of green moss. It was the first time I had felt moss's springy depth, and, as she showed me the tiny translucent leaves, whirled round soft green stems, it was the first time I had looked closely at what surely was an enchanted miniature forest.

Stella Susan Barnard Yeatts, my grandmother, pointed out bugs and butterflies, spiders and birds, mushrooms and flowers as we walked. She and my mother were my first mentors in the natural world to which, it seemed to me, Grandmother was intimately attuned. I don't recall ever talking to her about such things, but through the years when I heard stories about leprechauns or other "little people" of the forest, I always assumed that Grandmother would not only be able to see them, she would know their names and invite them for tea. I yearned to share what I considered her special connection to the non-human world. This was the grandmother I would always remember. But there are other memories as well, some extraordinary, some bewildering.

When I was a few months shy of five, my nine-year-old sister Nancy and I stayed in the country with Grandmother, so that our parents could celebrate their tenth wedding anniversary camping on our "forty," a quarter of a quarter section (a section being a mile square, or 640 acres) of woodland with a creek running through. My parents had bought it just to have a little piece of wildness, and it was only a day's drive from our western Washington home in Chehalis.

Early in the morning of our second day at Grandmother's, she came to the bedroom where Nancy and I were still sleeping. Speaking with a soft urgency, she recounted a dream that had jarred her awake. In the dream, our parents had been exploring a beautiful flowery hill, hiking, running, and hugging now and then. As Mother whirled and skipped downhill, she stepped in a hole. She sprawled down hard, and there she stayed, looking up at Daddy with pain in her eyes. "She broke her hip," Grandmother told us. "A man will come soon to take you to her."

Her dream felt like a dream of my own to my foggy, not-quite-awake brain, and that is the quality it retains as I now remember it. But in just a few hours, a man knocked on the door to say he had to take us home. Our parents had had an automobile accident, and Mother's pelvis was broken.

I remember almost nothing of Mother's recovery or the weeks and months that followed, until the birth of my sister, Beth, some fourteen months later. But I cannot forget Grandmother's dream. What kind of sensitivity is required to know, from miles away, not only when your child is hurt, but on what general area of the body? And how challenging would it be for someone with that kind of sensitivity to cope with the vicissitudes of life?

My most unsettling early memory of Grandmother took place when she was no longer living in the country. I was eight or nine and visiting in her big white house on the hill, perhaps a mile from where we lived. It was in the midst of World War II, and three of my uncles—Grandmother's sons—were overseas. All were conscientious objectors—in the military as non-combatants. Uncle Roy served as an army doctor, Uncle Ray a medical technician, and Uncle Foy was a Seabee. (Seabees were US Navy construction battalions, sent in before the troops to build roads, bridges, buildings, landing strips, and the like. Sometimes arms were available in case they were attacked, but generally, their only weapons were shovels, saws, and bulldozers.) Unlike my earlier visits with her, now Grandmother rarely smiled. Her face was pinched and she talked of worries I didn't understand. But I did understand the words, though not the concept, when she told stories of terrible plots contrived by some of her sons-in-law. As I think back on it, I'm guessing that she may have resented the inequity ("Why did they stay home when my boys had to go?"). But then I went home confused, asking my mother why Grandmother would think things that didn't square at all with my experience of these uncles. Mother furrowed her brow and pursed her lips but said little, other than to assure me that my instincts were sound.

My uncles came home at war's end, in reasonably good health if you don't count the malaria Uncle Foy picked up in the South Pacific or the untold psychic scars that all three must have borne. And Grandmother smiled a bit more. She made a number of moves, eventually living with one of my aunts in Montana. Before long, we heard she had been diagnosed with paranoid schizophrenia and committed to the state hospital.

All these years later, this still troubles me. There is no question that Grandmother was losing her grip on reality. And "paranoia" seems an apt description. But I still wonder about the diagnosis, and wonder even more if the illness could have been avoided, or if not, helped in some way more constructive than confinement and drugs.

Born in Patrick County, Virginia, in December 1880, Stella Susan Ann Barnard was one of her father's fifteen children. Jehu, her father, was a schoolteacher, and perhaps the person responsible for instilling in Stella a deep sense of the magic of education. The only story I remember about my grandmother's school days had to do with her willfulness. Every day when her teacher-father called roll, he read each child's full name from the roll book. Stella Susan Ann Barnard felt she had one too many names. So one day when Jehu was out of the room, Stella walked up to his desk, opened the book, and lined neatly through the "Ann." When her father next called roll he hesitated in the midst of her name, then read it as now entered. He never mentioned the change.

Her mother died before Stella's eleventh birthday, after giving birth to her tenth child. Jehu married again a year later, to sire five more children. I've heard few stories about that time in my grandmother's life, but imagining isn't difficult. A little girl is left motherless. Too young to bear it, she was still old enough to care for younger siblings. And then, so soon, another woman—a much younger woman—takes her mother's place in the household. From all I've heard, Virginia Alice, Stella's new stepmother, was a kind and dedicated wife and mother. I was told, for instance, that she routinely walked the mile from their home to the Barnard family cemetery, carrying buckets of water to care for new cedars hedging the plots of her husband's family's graves. My arms and shoulders throb thinking of it.

Still, it can't have been easy for young Stella. Along with the ache of missing her mother, and confronted by the feelings not only of having a newcomer usurp her mother's place but also her own, as she, the eldest daughter, had tried to fill the lady-of-the-house role, she also, at a most confusing time of life, had no one to ask questions to or confide in.

Stella had overheard women whisper about bad girls who got pregnant before marriage. When she began menstrual periods, with no understanding of what was happening, she thought somehow that the blood must mean she was pregnant, and therefore bad. She packed her bags, getting ready to run away from the shame. That desperate journey was apparently avoided or aborted midway—I never heard that part of the story—but I ached for that poor frightened and bewildered little girl.

In 1899, when she was nearly nineteen, Stella married dreamy-eyed Charles Thomas Yeatts and they quickly began a family. She gave birth to two sons and three daughters in Virginia. Then, in 1909, she and Charles Thomas moved their family to Montana, following some of Stella's Barnard relatives. En route, she had a gruesome miscarriage. (I was told that during the family's train trip west, a baby boy's head was born. "Just a head." I assume it had to be more than a head for it to be recognized as a boy, but "just a head" conveys the horror of the moment.) They began a cattle ranch in Beaverton, Montana, near Saco, where Evy, their two-year-old baby girl, soon died. Another son and two more daughters were born in the next five years.

After they settled in Montana's sagebrush, my grandpa still made business trips back to his rolling green Virginia hills. They had lived in the West nine years when in 1918, on one of those trips back home, he died at age forty-two, presumably a casualty of the flu pandemic. So Grandmother, at thirty-seven, became the sole parent on a ranch with seven children between the ages of three and seventeen.

From their births, Grandmother had steered her flock toward college. Now the challenge would be finding the money to keep everyone healthy without compromising their chance at higher education. So the oldest three took care of the ranch, helped teach at the high school, and found odd jobs. Starting at age twelve, my mother cooked, kept house, and cared for the young ones. My self-educated (after the eighth grade), brilliant grandmother hired herself out as maid and laundress, the only available way to bring in extra funds. Mother said that in her own job as chief chef, she provided a "balanced" diet: one day they would have bread; another day she'd find protein for the table; vegetables would appear on yet another day. She may have been exaggerating to make a point, but that point was that food was scarce, and difficult for a twelve-year-old to provide. What was available surely went to the children, though; I imagine Grandmother's fare was far more restricted.

So I always wonder, was it schizophrenia (diagnosed in her sixties) or malnutrition, or was it loss and stress? The loss of her mother, of babies and a husband, the anxiety of keeping her family healthy and on track for the education she valued so highly, fearing for the safety of her sons at war— all would take a toll on anyone. But mightn't it take a particularly intense toll on a very sensitive person—one who, it seemed to me, had not only a magical connection to nature but also a level of consciousness unattained by most of us?

And yet, I suppose her diagnosis and care were appropriate for that time, in that society, and with the medical knowledge of the day. In another period she might have been burned at the stake: I'm sure her unusual perceptions could be seen as proof-positive of witchdom. But there have also been communities who revered those endowed with unique vision or understanding. Instead of being drugged and shut away, she might have been the tribe's Wise Woman, whose insights would be sought out and valued. Or an enlightened society might have found nutritional or hormonal imbalances that could be treated, and given therapy to support, rather than deny, her character.

It haunts me. I certainly saw behavior that spoke of illness. And in later years I heard stories that made it apparent the family needed help caring for her. I just wish it could have been otherwise. She had so much to offer, and others gained much from her. To make college more accessible both physically and financially, she sold the ranch after her first four graduated from high school and bought a house in Missoula, a university town. Of her seven living children, six finished college (this was in the 1920s and early '30s), one becoming a medical doctor and three earning master's degrees. My Aunt Ellen, the one who didn't finish, preferred doing her own reading to attending classes. Though less formal, her education was likely comparable to that of her siblings. Grandmother's passion for learning, along with her transcendent spirit and excitement and curiosity about life, were passed down not only to her children, but to her children's children, and beyond.

Grandmother set a path that I've spent a lifetime exploring. Wanting to undo those last years, I fantasize that one day I'll come upon an emerald swath of moss and there she will be, eyes sparkling up at me, tossing her head with a laugh and an invitation to join her, exploring the woods.

Charles Thomas Yeatts, Stella's husband and my maternal grandfather, is a man who, like my father's mother, resides only in my imagination. He died more than seventeen years before I was born. I've seen photographs, heard a few comments, but rarely stories. I try to fill in the gaps and I come up with a multitude of unrelated men. His photos show a slight, dark-haired, sensitive-looking young man. He had the kind of eyes you could fall into. "Black cherry eyes," my mother used to say.

I asked Mother why he traveled so much, making those frequent trips back to his native Virginia from their Montana cattle ranch. She seemed uncomfortable with the question but answered, "He wasn't cut out for ranch work. He and his brother had a store . . . " She paused. "I think he was just more at ease in town." I felt there was much she wasn't saying, but it was apparent that was all I was going to hear.

Aunt Mary, my mother's older sister, didn't talk about their father either, but when the subject came up she would set her mouth and make a disapproving grunt. I thought she must have felt he had abandoned the family when he went east, and she had never been able to forgive him. Eventually I combined Aunt Mary's negative reaction with the fact that in young adulthood Mother had been a zealous member of the Women's Christian Temperance Union (WCTU), and I wondered if perhaps my grandpa had been an alcoholic, but I have no concrete reason to believe that.

Several years after my mother died, Aunt Ellen, Mother's next-younger sister, showed me a picture of a beautiful, solemn Native American woman holding a dark-eyed baby boy. Aunt Ellen said that she had just been told the baby in the picture was her father —my maternal grandfather, Charles Thomas Yeatts. I heard no stories about my great-grandmother, Caron Aquilla Boswell Yeatts. If she *was* Native American, Mother and her siblings would not necessarily have known. Or perhaps that information would have been suppressed. If Charles Thomas was half Indian, I don't know what that would tell me about his personality, but it could tell me something interesting about my own genetic makeup.

Later I got yet another picture from my Uncle Roy, the firstborn child of my Yeatts grandparents. When I visited him in Virginia after my parents' death, he showed me the half-log and plaster Virginia house where the family had lived until he was nine. Two doors were maybe eight feet apart, on one side of the house. Uncle Roy laughed and said, "Papa would play his fiddle and we'd all dance along behind, out one door and in the other, out and in, round and round, driving Mama to distraction."

I'd not imagined that side of him before: My grandpapa, the playful musician, the dancing papa. Doesn't sound much like a rancher, somehow. Perhaps it was part of the same coltish personality that enjoyed giving his children initials that spelled their first name. His tribe included Roy Oliver Yeatts, Foy Osmond, May Agnes (later to become Mary), Amy Maude (my mother), Evy Venice, Ray Alexander, Fey Ellen and Imy Mildred. My mother referred to the miscarried baby as Tom, but added, "Papa would never have agreed to that name."

Uncle Roy also told a heart-rending story that put an entirely different face on my grandfather's travels. He spoke of coming unexpectedly into the room where his parents were talking, seeing his father's head on his mother's lap, she gently stroking his hair. Uncle Roy heard his papa say, "Can't I please stay, Stel?" She smiled sadly and said, "There'd just be more babies." Separation seemed the only cure for so great a love.

So I don't really have a clear picture of my Grandpa Yeatts. Clearly he contributed to my foundation, but I'm not sure whether to attribute the mortar, the bricks, or the rods.

I wish I could have known him.

11

Framing and Closing

How happy those whose walls already rise!
—VIRGIL

Inside a house, your major relationship is with the floor. That's where you stand, walk, dance, set your furniture, lay the dog bed, or build block towers with the baby. When I used to put a ball on the floor in my house in town, it would roll diagonally to the far corner of the room. If the foundation isn't level, it's hard for the floor to be. Also, the floor will creak as you move about on it if it hasn't been carefully framed or if the plywood sub-flooring isn't firmly attached. A foundation that is strong and level, with the floor acting as a diaphragm across it, is necessary for the walls, stairs, and roof to be plumb and square. I've always been grateful that my personal foundation was a strong one. Now as I admire the crew's work, from carefully leveled form boards to the nailed sub-flooring and wall framing, I am grateful as well for the good start my house is getting.

With the upstairs sub-flooring laid, the crew, as they did below, uses the floor as a surface to frame the north, south, and east walls, which they then tilt up into place. The upstairs could be considered a large loft or balcony, the floor's west end stopping four feet short of the end of the house. The west exterior wall rises two floors, uninterrupted by first-floor ceiling or upstairs floor. This, therefore, will be a "balloon-framed wall," using continuous studs from the floor plate above the ground-level sub-flooring to the top plate below the roof, all built standing in place.

David and Curtis mark stud positions every sixteen inches along the floor plate. Then they add marks for the "king studs" (three studs nailed together), a structural requirement to protect against shearing stress. These will be attached to the vertical sides of the window frames and secured at their base to the foundation wall by the metal brackets called "hold-downs." Because the north and south walls are up, the men know where the eaves will be, so, knowing the angle of the roof slope, they measure, cut, and nail studs for the tall (twenty-four feet to the ridge), narrow (sixteen feet) west wall. A diagonal brace on the inside keeps the lumber in position. After several days of painstaking work, they sheathe the outside with structural plywood, making the wall stiff enough that the bracing can be removed.

A couple of weeks earlier, when they began to work on the second floor, Curtis had borrowed scaffolding from a contractor friend. This is ever more essential now that it is time to hoist up the glue-lam beams to support the roof. Eight 2x4s glued together make a beam approximately four by sixteen inches and twenty feet long, to bear on the king studs that are on each side of the big west window. The glue-lams each weigh about 240 pounds. Four men maneuver each beam into place as I stand watching with my mouth open. Then they place the 2x12 rafters, and the roof framing begins.

It is important to David and to me that the house has a small footprint on the ground in order to disrupt the hydrology and the natural communities as little as possible, so we are going up rather than out to find the other half of our proposed thousand square feet. As the house perches on a rather narrow bench on the hillside, the longer dimension of the house parallels the contours of the land, and because we intend to use the sun's energy for our electrical power, David chose this site, where that long front side faces south.

The mudroom on the southeast corner has its own roof peak, as do the entrance and the main room. This gives the east end of the house a triple crown, each steep roof a 12:12 pitch (meaning that the roof slope rises a foot for each foot along the horizontal plane). The slopes of the roof reflect the line of Douglas firs marching down the hillside beyond the house. It's one of my favorite views.

September 2008, the month of our fiftieth wedding anniversary. The air smells of blackberries and tarweed by the time the roof framing begins. Daylight arrives later, departs earlier, and is more frequently filtered through clouds. Now and then we cancel because of rain—not good for scrambling on sky beams. I nervously watch the calendar. Will we be able to get the house enclosed before the rains begin for real?

Equally nervously, I watch our bank balance dipping lower and lower, like a bucket with a not-so-slow leak. We need Curtis's energy, expertise, and steadiness to meet our deadline. But how much longer will we have the funds to pay him?

In spite of my anxiety, work progresses. The crew finishes framing the roof; they sheathe it with plywood, put flashing around openings and bends in the roof, and cover the whole thing in thirty-pound building paper. Then they wrap the walls in Tyvek, a moisture barrier that also slows air passage while allowing vapor to pass. Whew! Not uptown yet, but a dry spot to work inside, and a way-sturdier tent for the soon-to-come winter.

After the house is safely wrapped, the crew frames the stairway from the main to second floor. Since that walk-through when the foundation boards were first laid out, I had been waiting to experience the upstairs. Now, one, two steps and I look up to see a hawk sail by above the skylight. Three, four, five, six steps, a gnarly oak tree is perfectly framed out a window to the right. Seven, eight, nine, I see sky in a window above the framed oak, where at night will be stars. Ten, eleven, twelve steps, I'm face to face with another oak, its trunk far below. Step thirteen, turn, walk by the someday-bathroom and closet into the grand cathedral bedroom. To the north, I'm at ground level with the back hill. West, I look across a fifty-foot clearing to fir trees, once again at about my same elevation. But to the south, looking at treetops and beyond to distant hills, I get a tremendous rush. I always wanted a tree house, and now I feel as if I have one: if I walked outside and through the air about sixty or seventy feet, I would be in the canopy, just like the swallow now sitting at the tip of a Douglas fir. Far below I see a glimpse of the pond and our campsite.

As a special concession to my obsession with sleeping outside, David has designed a sleeping porch outside of that south wall. I can hardly wait: from there I should surely feel as though I were sleeping in the treetops.

Soon windows arrive and I begin to think we might really make it—might have the house under cover before winter. These are beautiful, expensive windows, and I hover over the unpacking, worrying that one will be cracked, or even worse, that we will drop one in the hanging.

This definitely won't be a glass house, but David planned each window's placement with care. The high glazing lets in maximum light; views are framed from what will be my upstairs working space, from the living room, from the bed; vistas open as you walk from place to place in the house. One of David's favorites is a shot straight through the house from a window in the east end of the mudroom, through the glazed door that separates the mudroom from the main living space, to a window in the great room that looks up the west slope. From inside I can appreciate the terrain as well as get a good peek at passing deer, or arriving guests. Narrow as the house is, there are almost no inside walls without natural light, so even without an extraordinary amount of glass, it feels very light inside—a distinct plus for those of us who tend to prefer outside to in, as well as saving electricity by rarely having to turn on lights in the daytime.

Once the windows are in, we turn our attention to a pile of logs Matthew saved for us when he was removing firs for our firebreak. These are decent-sized logs—a foot and a half or more across—that didn't have enough straight length to satisfy mill requirements. We think they will be perfect for siding the shed, and now call a neighbor who has a portable mill and lives just a few miles down Territorial Highway.

Jan, a tall, blond, Nordic-looking fellow, arrives at 8:30 a.m. sharp, pulling his Wood Mizer super hydraulic mill behind his big Dodge Ram. We let him know what we have in mind, and he pushes a log with his foot, rolling it down the bank to land beside his mill. He stabs it with his peavey, a long-handled tool with a spike in the end and a hook on one side, and rolls it onto the Mizer's fingers, which lift it onto the deck.

Now the log sits on an open-rail platform. With Jan's hands on the controls, the machine turns and slices the log into a sixteen-by-sixteen inch cube. He splits that in half, dumping the top half, and begins shearing off 1x8s, while a down-turned side pipe shoots out sawdust. Earlier log slices and the dumped 8x16 wait in the mill's down-slouched arm, cradled in its upraised metal fingers. When the saw reaches the end of the board, it backs up. As each board moves through, David grabs it, hauls it forward to catch its middle, and carries it to the pile. If the next one comes too fast, I grab it. Otherwise, I peer at the operation, taking notes.

Jan stands at the machine's control panel watching, directing. Levers guide and control the clamping arm; six levers move and position the log forward and back. The reverse lever is on the side. Liquid from a tank filled with water and soap drips onto the blade to keep it cool. The reserve 8x16 lifts onto the deck and—*whrrrr whrrrrr*—becomes another pile of 1x8s. A four-toothed jaw reaches up from below to rotate end pieces, flips them upright, and off comes the bark, as they too become 1x8s.

A new log tumbles down the hill. Jan stabs it with his peavey and spins it onto the Mizer's fingers, which lift it onto the deck. Six more logs become lumber, more than enough to side the shed. Possibly enough for flooring or maybe some ceiling in the house. I'm giddy. This is my first experience with home milling, and I wish we could build the whole house with our own milled lumber.

It's November and the birds have long been feasting on the dry brown seeds of the oceanspray. I can hardly believe our good fortune that the weather has been mild and dry enough to allow our project to continue. But it's framed now. It's getting closed up. There's hope!

We go to recycling stores shopping for used doors, to Steelhouse in Saginaw for brown metal roofing, and to Redwood Northwest for lumber, which we have rough-cut for board and batten siding. Curtis and his crew begin laying the roofing just as we get a call from Dennis, the neighbor with whom we share a well. We are all but out of water, he tells us, and will have to drill deeper. Dennis will make the arrangements and we will split the bill. Oh, man! Not timely when we're hoping to get maximum stretch from our remaining funds. But water is one thing we can't do without.

After the well drillers go down another hundred feet, they find water. Not a lot, but water. If they go deeper, they say, they will get into salt. So we stop, put in a new pump, and are glad our two families already added a two-thousand-gallon storage tank.

I check our bank balance again, which is now sorely depleted, and talk with Curtis. He finishes the roof and attaches gutters that will direct rainwater into two 1,250-gallon cisterns. If we collect the roughly fifty inches of annual rain that falls on the five-hundred square-foot area of our roof, we could have, according to my calculations, 15,652 gallons of water—plenty for irrigating, washing clothes, and toilet-flushing, and also enough that, with investment in more cisterns and requisite filters to keep it clean, we could use some for domestic purposes if the well doesn't hold.

Then Curtis nails siding on the east and west ends of the house and heads for his pickup. It is hard to tell him good-bye, but I am tremendously grateful that we were able to have him and his friends help us for as long as we did.

From here on out, it will be up to us.

12

What Makes a Home?

Where we love is home—home that our feet may leave, but not our hearts.
—OLIVER WENDELL HOLMES

Fall's red-splashed leaves are more and more frequently rimmed in frost, but I refuse to entertain any negative thoughts about living in our campsite by the pond. Though the house now looks like a house from the outside, the resemblance stops within the walls.

I hunch over the camp stove, waiting for it to heat my morning tea water. Together, the stove flame and the simmering kettle emit enough warmth that my shoulders begin to relax and my shivering slows a bit. When steam starts to escape from the spout, I pluck a couple of fir needles from yesterday's tea bag and pour hot water over it, watching mini-clouds form above the cup. Clutching the cup with both gloved hands, I lean my face close to breathe in the steam. When the cup gets too hot, I hold it between my knees, shifting it back to my hands again when my legs begin to feel the burn. Once the tea has cooled enough to drink, I take the kettle off the stove and put it on my lap, wanting to absorb every bit of its residual warmth.

The olive oil is solid, so I know the temperature is below forty degrees, but fir twigs bristle with dew—not ice. So it must be thirty-four degrees or so. I'd managed fine in colder. Still, I look inside our twenty-five-year-old Toyota wagon, parked beside the kitchen table, wondering about its bedroom potential. I have slept in it from time to time, but it seems overly cozy for two. For now, the leaking tent will have to do.

Standing by the car, I catch my reflection in its side mirror. Collars of two coats, one tan and one navy, a wool plaid shirt, and a bulky, turtleneck sweater all bunch under my chin, my head pulled down, turtlelike, within them. A brown wool watch hat peeks out beneath a fuzzy white cloche. Wisps of gray hair escape around the edges, testifying to my reluctance to bare my head to the cold for long enough to brush my hair. Blood-shot eyes surrounded by puffy flesh look out over a red nose, a lone drop about to slide from its tip.

"I look like a homeless person . . . Funny thing!" I snort.

It is now late November 2008. David and I have been camping by the pond most of the past year and a half, but we've never really considered ourselves homeless. Until seventeen months ago we had owned a house in town, although we rented it out. And for several years before that we at least had a dilapidated trailer to sleep and cook in when the weather was bad. But with time the trailer disintegrated: sections sank into the ground and exposed a nine-inch space that invited wildlife to find refuge. Battles between unidentified creatures and the paranoid occupant cat spewed papers across the floor, overturned containers, and knocked spice jars into the sink. Meanwhile, a garden of mold crept across the counters. We would eventually retrieve anything worth salvaging, but for now, we keep our distance, except to refill the cat's dish. And I'm not interested in sleeping there again, even as water rises on the tent floor and my fingers turn numb.

But for all that, we certainly aren't homeless. "Homeless" refers to people without anything, doesn't it? David and I have land and a garden, and are working on building a house. As I shiver under a fir tree, I stifle a humorless laugh, thinking of the old line about education being the path to success. So how is it that my inter-disciplinary master's degree finds me pondering the meaning of homelessness as I near age seventy-three? Yet in truth, I've always known that education came with no guarantees. My father graduated from law school and was admitted to the Montana State Bar in 1929. After the stock market crashed, he wandered Washington and Oregon with itinerant laborers, his hard-earned papers in his pocket as he shook prunes from their trees, harvesting them for the canneries. He fell in love with the lush, green Pacific Northwest, but no law firms there were taking on newly minted attorneys in the midst of a depression. Eventually he found a less-than-satisfying job in Seattle with an insurance company. Then in 1932, in a move that must have been as frightening as it was exciting, he took over the office and library of a retiring lawyer in the little town of Chehalis, Washington. He, with my mother and year-old big sister, rented a tiny house on stilts on Prindle Street, where floods lapped at the foundation each winter. But even in hard times people needed legal advice and found ways to settle their accounts. For his counseling my father was sometimes paid a jar of honey, a bag of potatoes, or the hindquarter of a pig.

As Daddy struggled—sometimes anxiously, but usually happily—to develop the career he loved, many whose success was measured in money abandoned hope, family, even life itself. As my sisters and I grew, Daddy often mentioned the absurdity of working—of spending one's life—for monetary gain alone. It had to be for passion.

In one of his syndicated columns, economist Paul Krugman, noting that computers excel at cognitive and manual tasks (including legal research and medical diagnosis) that follow explicit rules, said that too often now, college degrees are tickets to jobs that don't exist or don't pay middle-class wages. But for me, college education was never about job training. Rather, I would hope an educated person would be able to think independently, to evaluate what she hears or reads so that she'll not be led blindly, frightened unnecessarily, or be dragged flopping to shore after swallowing some unknown fisherman's bait. Shouldn't we have an educational system whose pupils study their home—the natural world—along with their places in it, who get an unbiased background in history, its mistakes and triumphs, and who have deep foundations in music, literature, and fine and performing arts? And how about training in some of the practical arts that help a person care for herself? I would love to have taken that shop class and learned some basic carpentry. Creative students who understand both the natural and political world, students who can dream as well as analyze, will be able to find or invent work that is personally rewarding and that contributes positively to the planet. That is not training for jobs that don't exist: It is development of human potential.

So through the years, with my father's words in my heart, I left jobs for which I had lost my passion and eventually found great joy living where I felt a part of the changing seasons—the return of hummingbirds, turkey vultures, wood warblers; flowers turning to fruit, green leaves transformed to gold and ruby.

But gold and ruby are in the leaves right now, and at the moment I am cold. It is all very well to warm the heart and soul with memories and philosophic ramblings, but it doesn't do much for the extremities.

Thawed a bit by the tea and the kettle, I decide to try to move my icy bones. A flash of a bird catches my eye, darting from twig to twig in a willow across the pond, gleaning invisible bits of breakfast. The edge of the pond is bare, though a few weeks earlier, squeaks and plops filled the air, as bull-frogs, startled by a visitor's presence, leapt from their sunning spots back into the water. A fat half-foot in body length, these living gargoyles sat on the bank looking haughty and a bit disgruntled until someone neared, then, like age-group breast-strokers at the sound of the starting gun, they sailed through the air and disappeared into the water. But days both short and cold sent the frogs to seek sanctuary in the mud until the return of warm weather. I, on the other hand, have no winter refuge, mud or otherwise.

Then it occurs to me that rather than standing around feeling sorry for myself, I could follow the lead of the active bird and get my blood circulat-ing, a sure way to warm up.

Hiking up the hill at the end of our road, I come upon mushrooms in a multi-tude of shapes and colors: orange fairy cups, black elfin saddles, mushrooms with gills and teeth and pores, some with white fringes around the edge, some nearly black and grotesquely contorted, colonies of tiny white mushrooms, big burgundy-colored ones, tan and gold and brown-paper-bag colored, red and plum and even nearly blue. At one spot the ground is littered with bits of tan, white, and mauve caps and stems where deer or perhaps elk—some kind of messy, feasting megafauna—contributed leftovers for the mini- and micro-crews to clean up. It reminds me of when our son and daughter-in-law expressed wonder that their friend's baby ate so sloppily while their own young son was meticulous. And then they caught their dog (who was *supposed* to be in the other room at meal time) eagerly polishing up under their son's high chair. The memory makes me laugh as I think of the many levels of potential visits to the mushroom crumbs—from rodents to slugs to beetles and microorganisms—and maybe even someone's beloved dog.

Golf- and tennis-ball-sized divots under fir trees show where creatures—perhaps flying squirrels—have been digging for truffles, putting to mind one of my favorite examples of nature's networking. In fall and winter, flying squirrels, along with many other small mammals, smell the strong fragrance of truffles, a major winter food. They dig and eat these small tuberlike fungal fruits and, as they travel through the forest, deposit spores that have moved through their digestive tracts unharmed. The spores germinate, forming un-derground fungal networks that connect to tree roots, augmenting the roots' ability to collect water and minerals while they grow more truffles to feed the next cycle. And as the trees grow, they provide shelter for the squirrels as well as for owls, a major predator of these small mammals.

We're all intertwined, I muse. *The squirrels and fungus, the trees and owls, bugs and slugs, rivers and wind and stars, babies in their high chairs and canine vacuums. What a system!*

On the way back down the hill, I come upon myriads of mosses. Moss like velvet, moss flat and featherlike, moss that looks like tiny trees, and some a woolly tangle like a poodle's back. I think back on the thick and springy feel of moss in the woods of Washington where as a child I lay beside my grandmother. How many forest creatures must make it their bed, or collect it to line their sleeping quarters? And other beds come to mind: I remember, on rare and cherished camping trips with my parents, watching them lay blanket-rolls on thick fir-bough mattresses. We slept deeply and awoke refreshed.

What makes a home? A place to sleep? Warmth? Something to care about? Connections? How wonderful that the definition of home need not be confined to the space between walls!

I know evening will come early back at the pond kitchen. Those who live outside must adjust their schedules to the tilt of the earth. To get anything out of the garden, I have to be able to see, and at this time of year that will be possible until only about 4:30.

I am astonished to find tomatoes—December is just around the corner, yet they are partly ripe and still solid—and I harvest three different kinds of kale as well. I retrieve a big onion from its current storage place (the back of the car), put on rice, and begin chopping onion and tomatoes. The beans have been simmering for an hour or two.

While I was away, David moved our tent inside the empty shell of the house-to-be, upstairs, into what will eventually be the bedroom. And after washing dishes, he used the still-warm dishwater to thaw the olive oil, wrapping the bottle in a thick bath towel once the oil was liquid. As I begin fixing dinner under a lantern's light, David builds a fire in the stone ring behind where the tent used to be.

Blue sky turns peach fading to opal gray, as if distant techies are playing with the stage lights. Fir trees' green becomes black, and a wisp of a waxing moon glimmers beyond the trees. We pull chairs close to the fire, watching logs glow red, swell, pop, turn darker. We eat relaxed, contented, warmed to the core.

With dinner so early, I decide there will be time to fix something extra. Maybe Patrick will stop by. Patrick, a young friend from Ireland, drops in occasionally. We met him through our friend Gwendolyn, when we were selling plants at her farm stand in the nearby town of Veneta. When Patrick visits, he pulls out his tent if the weather is warm or sleeps in his car when it is not. He roams the Pacific Northwest spring to fall, farming or doing odd jobs, helping people out, earning his way. He spends winters in Mexico or India or the Pacific Islands—someplace warm. For Patrick, the world is his home.

I will chop some apples from our tree into the cast iron frying pan, simmer them a bit with cinnamon and honey, and top it all with cake batter. Add a heavy lid, adjust the heat just so, and before you know it, I'll have an apple upside-down-cake fresh from our two-burner camp stove. If Patrick doesn't come by, maybe tomorrow I'll take the cake to town for the woman who sits with her cardboard sign on the corner of Hilyard and Thirtieth. Or perhaps for the guys who sleep under the rhododendrons by the Episcopal church.

As the fragrance of cinnamon and cooking apples fills the air, Pegasus begins to emerge from the now-dark southern sky. And there is Cygnus. Before I'm ready for bed, Orion will take his place, hunting as always. Basho said that the journey is home. I delight in the journey. It is good to be home.

13
On Giving and Receiving

It is when you give of yourself that you truly give.

You receivers—and you are all receivers—rise together with the giver on his gifts as on wings.

—KAHLIL GIBRAN

Now that the tent is upstairs we decide to set up the rest of our camp in the mudroom. With no insulation yet in the walls, the blocking (the horizontal spacers between studs) makes perfect, narrow kitchen shelves. For a brief time, I actually feel somewhat organized. The building inspector makes a wry comment about our having "a pretty nice campsite" and we appreciate his understanding, as it will be a long time before we'll be able to apply for our occupancy permit. At fourteen by eleven feet, the mudroom makes a commodious living space—at least far more comfortable in its proportions than the trailer. But as much as I appreciate its interim duty, it is its future that I find exciting.

I have looked forward to having a mudroom since we first walked through and envisioned it, when only form boards marked the space. Though now three dimensional the room is far from functional, but I jump in my time machine to review its exciting uses and potential.

We can be working outside in any kind of weather and will come into this wonderfully indestructible room where we will keep our boots and rain gear, work gloves and hand tools. From it we can get to the bathroom without muddying up the main house and scoot back outside, nobody being the wiser. Or we can hang the dripping clothes on a hook and ditch the boots, or throw our dirty clothes into the washer if we're ready to go inside for a while. And above it all is a loft where we can store out-of-season clothes or visiting great grandchildren. Such daydreaming helps keep me warm through the winter.

April 2009. Though the propane heater roars furiously, the half-built, two-story house doesn't heat up like the little trailer used to. Even when we work in shirt sleeves outside, now that winter is officially over, we put on hats and jackets when we come in, reminding us not so subtly that we oughtn't put off insulating forever. All those walls are ready and waiting: their studs and blocking call for insulation cut to fit and pressed into their spaces. So, when some dear friends say they want to do something for us, and ask what we would want done if they could put together a work party, it isn't too hard to come up with an answer. But we figure working with insulation is a bit like latrine duty: who would want to do it?

I love group projects, so even though I feel uncomfortable about being the recipient, I gratefully agree. Then they say they want to buy the insulation. "Oh no!" I complain. "I can't let you do that."

"It's done," Sandra says. And I shrink into the nearest deep dark hole.

I became especially close to Sandra and Ginny during the years that I worked at Hendricks Park, Eugene's beautiful rhododendron garden, after David's hemorrhage. Both of them are super-organized, so when they say something will happen, it's not just wishful thinking. Now we hear that they've gathered a gang that will appear in a few days to begin stuffing the walls. We know we should get ready for them, but what in the world does "getting ready" mean? Clearly we must empty out our "kitchen shelves"— the blocking in the mudroom walls—so the wall space will be available to insulate, but after that, how do we go about organizing a work party? As we waste time wondering, Jeff and Rachel arrive to help us in a test run. We four install the nasty yellow fiberglass insulation and at the end of the day we have scratched-up arms and hacking coughs, but we also have an insulated ceiling and loft above the mudroom. What would we do without our kids?

Ginny (chief honcho at Hendricks Park at the time) and Sandra (mover and shaker of Friends of Hendricks Park) bestow on us fat checks for insulation, provided by a diverse group of over two dozen angelic friends. After surviving the shock of that, we shop, and Sandra and Ginny show up not only with a crew to install it, but also with goodies to keep our internal motors revving.

For years I had envisioned having an old-fashioned barn raising, where a community of friends would gather and I would keep them fed and watered while we all worked. But before we started building, I heard about a house raising where, as the keg got lighter, the work got more questionable until the owner began to worry that rather than a house raising, he might have a razing. When one tipsy helper nearly fell from an upper floor beam, the owner called the party off. So I was more than a little anxious, early in our project, when I asked Curtis if he would be interested in supervising a group effort. He clearly was uneasy about choreographing an amateur crew to build the house, and as we weren't comfortable directing it ourselves, I gave up on the idea. But now the basic construction is finished, and here are willing, hard-working, organized folks prepared to do a job that is nobody's favorite. And they even brought food.

Ginny, Kate, and Kit cut pieces to shape and size. Beyond the top of the ladder, John scales the frames and pokes pieces in the walls and ceiling so high up it nearly makes my nose bleed to watch him. Linda, Fred, Sandra, and Judith, along with the cutting crew and David and me, pair up and measure, cut, and stick fuzzy rectangles of insulation wherever we can reach. A friend had told us about an insulation called eco-batt, made without the binders and chemicals that make conventional fiberglass insulation—the kind we used in the mudroom—so unpleasant to work with. These brownish batts are much more forgiving than the conventional stuff, but still, even with everyone in gloves and masks, I hear a few coughs and see some arm-scratching going on. They work until they ache and stomachs rumble, finishing all of the exterior walls downstairs, most of the twenty-four-foot-tall wall, the mudroom, and upstairs. All we have left to do is the stairway wall, upstairs ceiling, and above the crawl space under the house. We swell in admiration of a long day's work well done.

Then Sandra, Judith, and Linda spread out a feast.

I feel a colliding mix of gratitude and humility. If it is more blessed to give than to receive, these people are truly blessed. And I relinquish the last vestiges of any remaining illusion of being the master of my fate. For a very long time I've been aware that the self-made (wo)man is a fiction. How much credit can I take, for instance, for the fusion of that particular egg and that particular sperm that became me? And I doubt it had a lot to do with my personal ingenuity that got me born into the lush and still-somewhat-wild northwest corner of the Land of the Free. Or that I happened to be one of those in that land who actually *was* free. And so it continued throughout my life, as I learned in classes taught by someone far cleverer than I, read from books written by others, drove on roads that I did not build, drank clear water I had not formulated. I am grateful for each friend, each totally undeserved gift, each perk bestowed by civilization, community and the universe. Finally I understand monks having to give up all material things and beg for food. Acknowledge interdependence. Dissolve the big "I." Say thank you. Though I can set my course and choose my response, I am not sole master of my fate. And isn't it wonderful not to be alone on the road? "What I aspired to be, / And was not, comforts me," as Robert Browning said.

Late April and dogwood-blooming time: winter's chill is just a memory. New insulation blocks any bite that might try to revisit, and the blessings of friends warm our hearts. Sufficiently warm, unfortunately, that rather than finishing the insulation, we go on to other projects. I spend the rest of the spring and most of the summer in the garden; David plans and supervises field communications at university track meets.

One day I go to town for a while and come home to find that the tent is no longer in the bedroom upstairs. Also the futon that was our bed in the trailer is now in the living room. David has moved it from the trailer, but wasn't eager, big surprise, to haul it upstairs. Then, with space enough to move around in the bedroom, he built a magnificent scaffold of braced, peeled, five-inch fir poles supporting a platform about eight feet above the floor. The whole thing reminds me of a double-decker four-poster bed for a giant. With a ladder on each side of the room and the scaffold in the middle, we get back to poking insulation here and there during any extra moments. I balance shakily on a board spanning the four feet of space from the top of the short wall on the bedroom's west end to the tall living room wall, the board's ends resting on the top of the railing and the all-too-shallow bracing on the wall, and think of how easily and comfortably John had covered the bulk of that west wall, his lithe height and long arms bridging distances I couldn't even imagine. But I push in a few pieces to fit snugly in their assigned spots; the board ends remain on their perches, and I inch my way back without falling to the floor twelve feet below.

Then we check out the new bed. Lying on the futon in the living room, we look up into the full twenty-some feet of open space and windows in the west end of the upstairs as well as those on the first floor. At night I watch the moon arc slowly across the space—first low, midway in the patio door, then in the tall upstairs window at the west end of the south wall, and later, through panes of the big west-end window, also upstairs. I count stars as they appear and move: two diagonally in this pane, three scattered in the next; one, two, five, seven, eight in various sections of the big window. On a moonlit night in late October I watch silver-edged clouds scudding across the panes. Occasionally, even here inside, I can see the Milky Way. I don't really like the *idea* of sleeping downstairs. It makes me feel old and feeble. But the *fact* of it is a joy. I love looking up into the high space, and out the windows into the night.

So at night, the west end of the great room becomes our bedroom. In the day we fold up the futon to become a couch and move some concrete blocks and a plywood strip to make a coffee table halfway between the couch and a couple of Wassily chairs from our house in town—their leather and chrome anachronistic in our pieced-together interior. We place a bookcase from David's old office behind the chairs to divide what has now become a living room from the kitchen/dining space, where a plywood-topped card table stands in for a dining table.

We fuss at the house between other jobs. A little insulation here; cover the insulation with plastic there; fix the wiring; set up a kitchen beside the dining-card table where the real kitchen will someday be. For now we make do with sawhorses and boards, the camp stove and dish pans.

Fall comes and goes; temperatures drop. Nesting one morning in flannel sheets, under five layers of blankets and a sleeping bag, I wear two pairs of socks, tights and sweat pants, long-sleeved shirt, wool sweater, and sweat-shirt, all topped off with my fuzzy winter hat. Fog puffs from my mouth and nostrils, but I'm quite cozy. The thermometer in our house registers twenty-two degrees. An article in the paper says warming stations helped 250 homeless people the previous night, but another 1,000 were still in camps, tents, under bridges, abandoned sheds, cardboard boxes. The official outdoor temperature is seven degrees.

I look out the window at frozen ground and am grateful for the windows and the roof, the mostly insulated walls, the sub-flooring that, though still not insulated, is out of mud and off the ice. I appreciate my half-built house and my husband, who is firing up the propane tank heater. Nonetheless, I am reluctant to get out of bed.

Mostly the winter doesn't continue to be that cold, but as soon as the ground is thawed and dry, I climb down the ladder to the root cellar, wriggle between the studs into the crawl space, and begin stuffing batts beneath the floor. Under most of the house, the crawl space is about forty inches, so rather than actually crawling, I walk bent from the hips, thinking of *Being John Malkovich*, the surreal and hilarious film where out-of-work puppeteer Craig Schwartz—John Cusack's character—finds a job as a file clerk on floor seven-and-a-half in the Merton-Flemmer Building. The half floor, his boss explains, "saves overhead." Bent at forty-five degrees, I try to assume the matter-of-fact attitude of his co-workers. Just another day at the office. Doesn't everybody walk this way?

Eventually I get most of the floor under the living area insulated. When my back starts yelling at me, I abandon the half-floor attitude and "walk" instead on my knees, which are well protected by gardening kneepads. With that insulation in place, we are immediately rewarded by milder house temperatures. We begin tacking screen-door fabric over the insulation to keep it in place and to discourage mice from using it as nesting material, then abandon the job once again, to be rescued some months later by our dear granddaughter Celina and her sweetie Geoffrey, who together finish the much-less-roomy space under the mud room and tack up the remaining screening. Rather than mimicking the cast in the John Malkovich movie, I imagine six-foot Geoffrey slithering on his back like an upside-down snake, and, though about my size, Celina's body-attitude is probably similar in that approximately thirty-inch space.

Celina, Jeff's daughter, is our oldest granddaughter of three; the younger two, Tasha and Camila, are Erika's and live in Flagstaff, Arizona. Celina and her big brother Nate have spent time here from their earliest years. I remember not yet two-year-old Nate playing in a pile of dirt in the new pond excavation, before the pond filled with water. Celina started visiting when she was riding in a pack on someone's back. And eventually, it was here—in a wonderful structure they built in the woods—that she and Geoffrey began their life together. They have been helping us from the get-go.

Now, with the floor insulation finally finished, we live quite comfortably in the 420-square-foot main room of the house, kitchen at one end, dining next, and living-room-by-day, bedroom-by-night at the other end. Adding the entry vestibule, small study, and bathroom, the space comes in at about 500 square feet, which feels more than adequate. The rest is just gravy. Lovely, but gravy.

14
Perfection

I spent a good share of my young life in the top of a willow tree. I looked down on my parents' rose garden and grape arbor, down on my long-roped swing hanging from a bar high in fir trees, a swing that could send me flying in long looping arcs. I looked down on lawns and apple trees and a huge vegetable garden; on pastures, woodlands, and hills in the distance. I ran barefoot all summer, listened to stories before bedtime, and sang songs around the piano with my family. My parents held hands when they walked together in the garden. They listened to each other's stories and laughed at each other's jokes. They showed us what love looked like as well as how it felt. As I approached adolescence, knowing that I wanted to be a writer, I began to worry that I would have nothing to write about—no parental neglect, no abuse, no drugs—no grist for the mill. Alas, for an author's future, my life was without angst.

Recently several women friends were discussing their childhoods and each described having to overcome the effects of parental foibles. I felt almost guilty that I couldn't join in. I somewhat apologetically remarked that my parents weren't perfect, but they were pretty good.

I play that discussion over in my mind and begin to wonder what my comment that "they weren't perfect" really meant. Not perfect according to whose criteria? If I get a perfect score on a test, it is a test written by someone who determines the correct answers. My perfect score indicates that my answers matched what the test-maker had in mind. Why should I judge my parents, or anyone, according to someone else's exam? And is a perfect score a reasonable goal, even on a test of my own making?

One summer a few years back I was annoyed at my less-than-perfect gardening when I had neglected to pull the bolted *Brassicas* (the cabbage relatives) on schedule. *Behind as usual*, I thought. *I'm glad none of my Good Gardener friends are looking over my shoulder.* Then because the part of broccoli and cauliflower that we eat are the plants' nascent buds, I decided to sample the flowers of collards, kale, and turnips—and decided we could get another tasty month out of them. A hummingbird darted into the garden to sip nectar from the kale flowers, followed close behind by a swallow-tailed butterfly. What a gift! Why did I need to feel my gardening wasn't meeting acceptable standards? Ever since, I have left a few kale and collard plants to flower, and some to seed, providing nectar for the pollinators and saving myself the trouble of buying new.

I read somewhere that mistakes are the first step to creativity. I love that thought. Those of us who grew up feeling the need to be perfect were often afraid to explore the unknown, missing the heights as we tried to avoid the depths. Our artist-grandson Nate became aware of that problem when he was in design school. Talented young men and women, accustomed to success and praise, were reluctant to risk imperfection in someone else's judgment by trying something different. But without being willing to risk failure, they might never discover just how creative, how *good*, they could be, or how much fun it might be to explore new ways of imagining. Still, risk-taking is scary. It can make a professional appear to be an amateur—humbling, but not necessarily bad. Amateur, from the Latin *amare*, to love, is literally one who loves what she is doing. And what's not to admire about that?

Recently an art critic praised an artist's stunningly lifelike paintings of flowers, saying that the painter was in a class apart from the many who paint flowers or sunsets and shouldn't. *Shouldn't?* So maybe they'll never get hung at MoMA, but *shouldn't?* You shouldn't sing unless you'd be invited to the Met? Shouldn't run unless you can break a four-minute mile? Shouldn't write a newspaper column unless you've won a Pulitzer in journalism? This view presumes judgment—by self or critic—to be more important than joy, and precludes apprenticeship, experimentation, and risk-taking by professionals as well as by amateurs.

When I was in landscape architecture school, I frequently found it difficult to turn in a project because I always felt I could do more, do better, bring it closer to perfection. These many years later I still want to do the best I can, because it feels good. I want to plant beautiful gardens, grow healthy plants, prepare nourishing food. I want to walk fast and breathe deeply and write sentences with both meaning and grace. I want to live fully and with compassion. Still, daily I ask myself forgiveness for attaining less than my former—or perhaps even present—ideal. But I remind myself to aim for the best I can do in this particular moment—with this much energy, this many distractions—not what might be possible with a personal coach and eight hours of daily practice, or what I could have done when I was twenty-five, or what rich and famous superheroes do or dictate.

In theory, I no longer strive for perfection. "Perfect," etymologically, means "completely finished." I am not finished. And I don't want to be constrained by the rules of someone else's exam. I want to live—to experiment and experience—to sing and draw flowers, to run, garden, and write imperfectly. I want to accept that it is partly my unique failings that make me who I am. I don't need memories of childhood angst for writing fodder. What angst we don't create for ourselves, the world creates for us. It gives us a lifetime of material to explore. I want to appreciate the imperfection in others as well, to learn more, to explore other roads. I don't plan to be completely finished, even when I die. I want to decompose and recycle my nutrients to some other imperfect life. And I don't want my grandchildren to debate the degree of my imperfection. I want them to say, "She got enormous joy from life."

I'd like to think the past is truly "completely finished," so it might as well be considered perfect. But of course that is total fiction. It's starry-eyed, mushy-brained, wishful thinking. It's a good line, perhaps, for assuaging guilt. (*That is so yesterday! Get over it! Today is a new day.*) But the apple tree pruned to the wrong bud will flaunt its crooked branch forevermore, unless I cut the whole thing off. Yesterday's pollution acidifies the oceans today and tomorrow and tomorrow, killing plankton—that essential food of fish—and dissolving skeletons of coral and carapace of myriad shellfish. Today's mistakes, like today's extravagant purchases, will be billed to our grandchildren, perhaps crushing them under their weight.

The Black Plague revelers said they would "eat, drink, and be merry, for tomorrow we die," and perhaps as death waited behind the door, that was the best way to live those last moments. But the slash-and-burn folks—the exploit and leave, clear-cut and move farther west, blow up one mountain and look for another folks—could also be said to be living in the moment. I am dumbfounded by the space-exploration advocates whose rationale is that once we finish destroying this planet, we need another to colonize. If the past is perfect, we learn nothing, and therefore are prepared to continue our destruction somewhere in outer space.

I do believe in living in the moment, as in being attentive, awake, grateful for what is here, today. The moment, after all, is the only place we can live. Still, the effects of yesterday remain, as does my responsibility to tomorrow. The past is present. Today and tomorrow build on yesterday. I hope I can not only smell the balsam in the air this beautiful day, feel the breeze's cool breath on my skin and all ten of my toes curled into the ground, but can also see that crooked branch in the apple tree (or thoughtless words uttered, those of comfort left unsaid). There's no point in sackcloth and ashes once it's done, but if I see what is, and why it is, and what the cut was that caused it, perhaps I can learn something, and do better next time.

Learn from the missteps; cherish the memories, but let go. One summer day David climbed onto the tractor, engaged the mower, and mowed down the remains of the display garden, watching bits of penstemon and heliotrope flash briefly by, among blackberries, thistles, and wild roses. More than two decades ago I conceived of this Jekyll-inspired garden in love, as a carefully orchestrated rainbow of color: red, orange, yellow, green, blue, indigo and violet, with a few contrasting colors sprinkled here and there for harmony or emphasis. Both exciting to plan and to execute, it had a season or two of beauty before David's cerebral hemorrhage and my resulting job change shifted my attention away from the garden, letting rogue plants thrive while those we wanted succumbed to competition and unmet needs. Here was a Buddhist lesson in non-attachment: the garden had been a delight to create, a joy to behold (briefly), but now it was gone. Thank you and farewell.

Both separately and together, David and I have visited some of our past projects: buildings he designed, gardens I made. Sometimes they still exist and look good, particularly the buildings. But many—most—have been neglected or obliterated, or, as when new paint is daubed over an old oil painting, have been unrecognizably altered. It doesn't make me sad, really, but puzzled. Perhaps old clients moved from a residence garden, or changed jobs from the clinic or apartment complex they once wanted designed. Maybe they got sick, and couldn't afford help. But what does it matter, really? These gardens gave me pleasure in the making and gave the clients pleasure in the receiving. They weren't intended to be monuments.

It's an odd feeling, though, seeing your creation—something you gave mind, muscle, heart, and a chunk of your life to—erased. You want to go look in the mirror to be sure you're actually still here yourself. Or are you peering back in time from the Great Beyond? Yet the joys of garden making are threads in the fabric of life. It's a song sung, its notes floating away with the breeze. Maybe all of life is performance art, measured in the living of it, not in its products. And certainly not in their perfection.

Friends ask when our house will be finished. I want it to get it to the point where we are warm and dry (roof, walls—check; insulation—check; wood-stove—working on it); have electricity (photovoltaic panels—check); have a functioning kitchen (well, sort of); storage (needs work); cleanable surfaces (nope)—but I don't even think about finished.

From 1976 to 1991 we remodeled our house in town. We moved the stairway, added a deck and balcony, remodeled the kitchen. For two years I did dishes in the upstairs bathtub because the kitchen was torn apart. As our daughter pointed out, we "changed every room" and were not particularly speedy about it. We came closer to completion when we rented it out, and closer still before we sold it, but we never really finished it. The architect remodels the remodel. *This space doesn't work as well as I had hoped. If we just opened it here* . . .

I've been asked how I put up with a half-built house and I wonder, where is it written that the greatest happiness comes to her who has all the molding installed? Did the wedding vows guarantee a finished house? Life from a page in *House Beautiful*? Would I have wanted them to? Seems to me that in this, as in all things, I have three choices: I can blame someone, which immediately makes me a victim, and therefore powerless; I can deal with the situation myself, in which case it has to be a sufficiently high priority that I give it the time and effort it demands (and in the case of the house, now that we are protected from the elements, the details aren't that high a priority to me); or I can accept, and enjoy, even less-than-perfect circumstances as they are. Meanwhile, I thank my lucky stars that the man I married has the talent and training to design this wonderful, even if never finished, house.

David is a poet and the house is his poem. I tinker with words, the length and flow of the lines, the feeling evoked by the writing. David tinkers with space and materials, balance, proportion, and there too, evoked feeling. He second-guesses, revises, looks from all angles—when it's on paper and when it's on the ground. When is a poem finished? At some point the poet stops one to begin another. Still, how often, picking it up five years later, does she not want to change at least one word?

Redwood boards and battens emphasize the tall and narrow dimensions of the house. The three peaks above two stories of mudroom, entry porch, and main section bring to mind a minicastle. To the right of the front door, the root cellar is still wrapped in Tyvek, waiting for its siding and for weather warm enough to glue on the rubber barrier that will support its green roof. To the left (south) of the main house, a foundation sits empty, awaiting the moment we have time and money to build an attached greenhouse. There I will start garden plants, grow citrus, ginger, and green tea, and will have a place for drying clothes even in the winter. But in between the future greenhouse and the unfinished root cellar, our house's redwood siding pushes to the sky, where roof gables create a silhouette against the tall fir trees and the roof's slope reflects the angle of their descent.

The house is far from completely finished. It will change. It will grow. But even now, it's a beautiful poem, if only just begun. If only still and always, imperfect.

15
Mudroom

We abuse land because we regard it as a commodity
belonging to us. When we see land as a community to which
we belong, we may begin to use it with love and respect.
—ALDO LEOPOLD

Our mudroom is our energy center. It is the home of the solar power controller, inverter, and batteries. Solar modules on the roof collect the sun's energy with which the controller charges deep-cycle batteries that store power for when the sun isn't shining, and at the same time protects them from being over-charged. The inverter then converts that power from direct current into alternating current for our household use. We have four 195-watt solar modules, giving us a nominal 780 watt-array capacity. It allows us to have a modicum of electricity without having to connect to the grid and it doesn't let us forget what we learned about conservation during the seventeen years that we had none. We turn on the lights when we need them—a real thrill, which it wouldn't have been our first fifty-seven years of life. One of the things I love most about our long camping venture is being able to appreciate things I once took for granted. It's like a sunny day in November or February. That's no big deal in Arizona, but in western Oregon, we break out our party hats. That's how I feel now when I flip on a light switch. When someday I get water out of a faucet, I may declare a national holiday.

With our four panels I run the computer, as well as occasional lights. We power a few other things (David's electric coffee grinder, the DVD player, the charger for our headlamps and radio batteries) for brief periods now and then. I think of our electricity as being like water in a bucket: if we steadily pour, even very slowly, from the bucket, we can easily empty it. But if we pour a dab now and another later—only when we need it and only as much as we need—we won't empty it before the next day when we have a chance to fill it up again. Winter 2009 to 2010, the first winter our photovoltaic system was in, we had to use the gasoline-powered generator to recharge the batteries only twice—once in December and once in January—running the generator for about a half hour each time. But by the second winter we'd learned how to conserve enough that the generator was never necessary. (We have since learned that even though their wattage doesn't appear to be low, some batteries need to be "stirred" by the generator periodically.) The inverter requires 1.7 watts of electricity to run its electronics and cooling fan, so we turn it off at night and use candles and headlamps for light as a rule, turning the inverter back on only when we need a few minutes of overhead light, or if I need to recharge my computer. We've been incredulous to see the panels charging the batteries on the shortest, foggiest, wettest Northwest winter days, and believe that if we chose to have a more extensive array with an equal investment in batteries, we could be downright profligate with our electric usage, except in the depths of winter. Fortunately for our pocketbook, we've never felt the need or desire.

What we do feel is comfortable—we have everything we require, though we may eventually get a small chest refrigerator for summer use, and perhaps a solar pump to get water from the pond. But we'll never have to pay a utility bill, or worry about our electric lights adding carbon dioxide, sulfur dioxide, or mercury to the air, which electricity from oil or coal so infamously does, or worry about power outages in stormy weather. I read that if an area the size of Manhattan Island were covered with solar panels, the entire energy consumption of the United States could be solar powered (*Alternative Energy Sourcebook* 1992)—at least, assuming someone solves the problem of storage. Let's hope we can find a way to do that before we blow off more mountaintops for coal or fight more wars for oil.

Some of our travelling friends say that the little bathroom by our mudroom replicates the size and arrangement often used in space-conscious Europe. You walk into the center of the three- by nine-foot room, right through the three-inch depression that is the shower pan. A washbasin with an overhead medicine cabinet will fit perfectly in one end, the toilet in the other.

Our toilet is ordinary looking and legally plumbed, but we won't use drinking water to flush it. The sanitary systems used by Western societies seem to me wrong on so many counts. First is the clear misuse of a precious commodity. A mere .01 percent of the planet's water is fresh; around two billion people have no access to clean fresh water; and Americans currently use 40 percent of potential drinking water "to transport shit," as a composting-toilet advocate so eloquently put it.

Gray water does the job nicely without flushing away the pure and potable. I used to watch my mother clean and flush the toilet with the used mop water, so I early learned the basic mechanics of a bucket flush. We have a very low-tech filtering system: we pour used bath or dishwater through a straw-filled twelve-inch plastic flowerpot into a five-gallon bucket that stores the now-cleaner water for flushing. After a few filterings, we add the nutrient-filled straw to the compost pile. We came up with this method after some unpleasantly stinky whiffs wafted through the house: we discovered that stored gray water quickly becomes putrid as bacteria feast on the bits of food and sloughed cells, feast and multiply and die, becoming food for more of their rapidly growing family. But filtering removes most of the bacteria's banquet and saves the goodies for the compost rather than the septic system. And a fresh filter magically transforms the room aroma from *eau de* dog vomit to the sweet summer smell of new-mown hay.

A five-gallon bucket filled with sawdust collects our urine and that of any visitors who feel comfortable using it. When the sawdust is nearly saturated, I mulch plants with it (not too close, to avoid burning them), giving them a good shot of nitrogen fertilizer plus a healthy dose of phosphorous, potassium, carbon, and calcium. As an extra bonus, while the enriched sawdust feeds the plants, it scares away the deer. When plants have as much as they can use, the soggy sawdust goes on the compost pile.

It's a wonderfully simple and serviceable system, and it makes me feel good, but I took awhile getting there. I was brought up in a society where not only did people not talk about money, race, or religion, they for sure didn't talk about bodily secretions or excretions. I was maybe forty when a nurse friend announced, as we left a public restroom, that she needn't wash her hands because her pee was far cleaner than the well-maintained bathroom fixtures or the door handle. That was a revelation to me, but researching it further not only confirmed her comment, it introduced me to the fact that Gandhi and others sometimes *drank* their urine. That still makes me shudder, but I accept as reality urine's cleanliness (if its host is healthy) and its beneficial properties. And I have learned much more about this most unmentionable (though what is more universally natural through the entire animal kingdom?) of subjects.

Squandering pure water is just one of the crimes of what we call "waste management." Another is the very fact that we consider it waste. Some scientists are awakening to the potential of biomimicry to solve myriad problems, learning from nature how to make better lubricants, solvents, self-cleaning surfaces, things like adhesives that mimic gecko feet, high-rise buildings that heat and cool like termite mounds and counter tops patterned after bacteria-resistant shark scales. Some designs featured in a recent *Sierra* magazine include solar collectors whose surface structures are based on that of a leaf, the new design absorbing six times the infrared light of the old flat surface; a solar cell inspired by the scaled surface of butterfly wings, used to produce clean-burning hydrogen; and a large solar plant whose design was patterned after the angles and spiral arrangement of sunflower seeds. Nature can be among our most important mentors, with applications to our sanitary systems being prime candidates. Cycles in nature involve production, growth, consumption, and decomposition. A seed germinates. The plant takes energy from the sun to make carbohydrates that give sustenance not only to the plant but also to the animals that feed on it and to other animals that feed on those. The plant drops its leaves on the ground; herbaceous parts die and return to the earth; the animals excrete unused metabolic products that become food for other organisms; everything that is living dies and is decomposed by organisms that release stored nutrients into the soil, where new seeds can germinate and new lives can grow. Nothing is depleted; nothing is wasted; nothing need be added from outside the natural cycle.

Andrew Moldenke, soil scientist and entomologist, calls soil "bug poop" because the metabolizing of macro- and microorganisms is the last step in the decomposition process. But the whole cycle is necessary. If you take out a single step, the cycle stops working. If organic material is removed from a field without being returned as compost; if the soil is sterilized, which kills invertebrates and microorganisms; if mineral soil is washed away in irrigation or rainfall on logged-over hillsides—the cycle is broken. "Round and round and round she goes. Where she stops, nobody knows," the carnival barkers of my childhood used to cry. But put a stick in the spokes, and— *whang!*—she stops. If enough of the wheels of fortune stop, everybody knows. Civilizations rise and fall with the fertility of their soil and the purity of their water.

If the cycle is complete, notably including the recycling of decomposing organisms and excrement of the living, the soil needs no fertilizer added to its natural compost. Yet we pipe away a good quart of urine per person per day, plus however many gallons of water to flush it down. New low-flush toilets use half or less of the three gallons per flush that used to be required, but all told, millions of gallons of water still are leaving any area that has a centralized sanitation system. Water tables drop measurably when a place changes from local septic to piped-away sewage systems.

Because bacteria flourish in water, water-based systems rapidly multiply the bacterial load, necessitating strong chemicals to counteract. Then the chemical soup, including resistant bacteria and viruses, gets dumped into our streams, lakes, and oceans, killing aquatic organisms and ecosystems. If we ship out our water, polluting water sources as we do it, and ship out our excrement, we diminish both the quantity and purity of the water and the fertility of the soil. We extract, consume, pollute, and waste. And as a bonus, we get to drink chlorinated water.

Sim Van der Ryn, emeritus professor of architecture at the University of California Berkeley and California State Architect in the 1970s, quoted a 1974 article noting that 335 million gallons of Los Angeles effluent was discharged into the Pacific Ocean each day. Van der Ryn calculated that 335 million gallons would hold enough nutrients for two hundred tons of 7-14-12 fertilizer (7 percent nitrogen, 14 percent phosphorous, and 12 percent potassium), each ton being enough to fertilize twenty-five tons of vegetables. So each day the city's "waste" (Van der Ryn prefers to call it "misplaced resources") could have grown five hundred tons of produce, sufficient for a pound or two of fresh vegetables per day for each resident. And that was in 1974. Imagine what it would be today.

Earth's population is projected to reach nine billion by 2050, and feeding all those people is a subject of worry, proposals, and argument. Most commercial fertilizer is petroleum based. How will we manage to fertilize the countless acres of required crops as petrol gets scarcer and more expensive? But have any of the planners realized that nine billion people would produce approximately nine billion quarts of liquid fertilizer per day (to say nothing of the solids)?

Some of Western society's reluctance to consider excrement as a resource grows from a general squeamishness about body processes. Joseph Jenkins, author of *The Humanure Handbook,* says we not only don't like talking about it, we don't even want to think about it, so we "defecate in our drinking water and then pipe it off for someone else to think about." Many people assume that flush toilets and sewers are essential for combating intestinal diseases like cholera and typhoid. But in fact, death rates actually rose when water-based sanitation systems were first introduced, because water distributes the bacteria. It wasn't until water supplies were carefully protected from fecal contamination—mostly through chemical sterilization—that these diseases were decreased. Bacteria in water grow and spread, but human "waste" decomposed by natural cycles returns its nutrients to the soil. Dust we are to dust returneth. There is no "away." Everything ends up somewhere, planned or not.

For centuries, Asian countries prized "night soil" as necessary for agriculture. Stories tell of farmers competing to build the most beautiful roadside privies in hopes of attracting wandering tourists to contribute to their stores. But Western culture has preferred an out of sight, out of mind approach, understanding neither what we are losing in water and nutrient nor what damage we are causing.

Nance Klehm, a Chicago landscaper and ecologist, recruited twenty-two community members to defecate into 5-gallon buckets rather than their toilets and bring her the buckets at the end of three months. The contents were dumped into fifty aerated 32-gallon garbage cans and stored for eleven months, when the garbage cans were emptied into a pile and the contents composted with comfrey leaves and old straw. A year later, Klehm delivered fluffy compost (which tested negative for fecal bacteria) to the participants, in two-pound bags labeled "The Great Giveback." *Mother Earth News* quotes Klehm, "It got people thinking more consciously about their personal connection to land, the cycle of food, water use, municipal treatment and human health."

As most of the nutrients in human excrement (up to 90 percent of the nitrogen and half of the phosphorus) are in urine, we feel pretty good about our current pee-in-the-sawdust-bucket routine, but still plan to build a composting toilet near the garden. The simplest version would be a toilet-seat-covered bucket with sawdust in the bottom and another container of sawdust or other organic material beside, so that each use is covered with the organic material. When the bucket is filled, it can be emptied onto the compost pile, along with food scraps and other compostables. Scrub the bucket with rainwater or gray water, with a little vinegar or soda if necessary, and pour the liquid on the pile as well, or under a well-mulched plant. It is important never to dump the wash water where it might get into a waterway.

Though it is true that if I am carrying no intestinal pathogens, none will spontaneously emerge from my humanure compost, to avoid having to request medical certificates from guests and to be absolutely sure of the fertilizer's safety for use on food crops, composting it for two years is recommended. I'll need at least two and preferably three bins to separate more or less finished compost, and I'll need always to have cover material (straw, leaves, clippings) readily available. I also plan to import fungal spores to assist in the decomposition process. I could, of course, use such a system in the house, but I know from carting our sawdust buckets that it's a bigger chore than I want to take on, at least right now when the compost pile is by the garden, a quarter of a mile or so away from the house. So for the time being, we'll use our sawdust bucket and conventional toilet when we're in the house and, when necessary, will flush with gray water to the septic system.

But will all of this effort do any good for the biosphere? I had a dispute with a fellow I met at a conference about the efficacy of individual endeavors to solve environmental problems.

"You can't stop global warming by recycling and changing your light bulbs," he argued, stressing the necessity of making sweeping changes in public policy.

My contention was that while of course appropriate public policy is critical, the world's human population is made up of individuals. If we each stopped buying gas-fired automobiles, for instance, or even just refused to buy a vehicle that gets less than eighty miles per gallon, or if we each stopped eating meat from big methane-producing feed lots, you bet it would make a difference.

But in the case of recycling gray water and using composting toilets, public policy and technology are essential. It is unrealistic to think that each of us would do jobs that range from laborious to disgusting. They are good methods to know about, though, for emergency situations. Earthquakes, hurricanes, and floods are just some of the possible causes of power outages, water shortage, or floating sewage in flooded streets. Instead of letting the toilet fill and stink, we can flush with dishwater. Or we can use five-gallon buckets and sawdust and bury the contents. But meanwhile, let's push for waterless sanitary systems at the neighborhood or community level, systems that will compost and give back to the earth, completing the cycle while we save water and eliminate one more potential for polluting it. An organized, cooperative community could provide numerous services, such as sanitary systems or solar electricity, that would be difficult or excessively expensive at the individual household level.

Eventually technology may bring us systems that can be used individually. The Gates Foundation is spearheading research for safe, clean, inexpensive waterless sanitation to address the serious health challenges faced by nearly 40 percent of the world's population, people in developing countries who currently have no or inadequate sanitary networks. They are researching methods to capture, treat, and recycle human waste, and have come up with ways to turn it into electricity, fuels, fertilizer, and pure water. An award-winning solution from Cal Tech features a solar panel powering an electrochemical reactor that turns excrement into hydrogen and fertilizer. In time, with Bill Gates pushing it, we may even accept sanitation as a reasonable and necessary topic of conversation.

Another principal player in the mudroom is our magnificent washing machine. After nineteen years of doing hand wash or trekking to the Laundromat, it's a thrill to have a machine of our own. But ours is not just any washing machine: it doubles as an exercise center. Through our nearly two decades of living without electricity, we thought a lot about alternative ways to do what needed doing, such as using rechargeable batteries, wind-up flashlights, and occasionally, a generator. But lack of space in our tent or trailer put a damper on large-scale experimentation. Our mudroom gives us space for a washing machine, but we wanted one that would not increase the demands on our solar panels.

I kept picturing my mother's wringer washer. It plugged into a light socket, using only a small amount of electricity. After the clothes had agitated long enough, we would squeeze them through the wringer (two rubber rollers) that we operated with a hand crank, and from there they would go into rinse tubs, and, after the final rinse, out on the line. Mother washed white clothes first, following with light-colored, then dark, each using the original water, each getting clean. She could do three full washer loads, using less than forty gallons of water. I wanted to copy the system, but power it with my own muscles rather than electricity.

Neil Kearns, long associated with Aprovecho Appropriate Technology Center and now with the Center for Appropriate Transport, wasn't able to find a wringer washer for me, but he designed a pedal-powered setup for a conventional washer. For the agitation cycle I back-pedal, and I pedal forward to spin the water out. I fill the machine and rinse tubs from the rainwater-collection cisterns, lifting the water with another human-powered machine, this one a pump, powered by pedaling a stationary bicycle. Once I carried buckets of algae-tinged water from the pot-garden storage tank, putting a new twist on the idea of green living. Maybe we can get our clothes to photosynthesize when they're hanging in the sun to dry.

The idea amused me, but the clothes seemed perfectly clean once they dried. Algae should not be an issue, though, if we filter water from the gutters and keep the tanks covered, which we're increasingly diligent about. Early on when we were more lax, storage tanks were a convenient habitat for mosquitoes as well as an occasional last dip for some hapless mouse. But covered tanks and gutters kept clean and screened provide hundreds of gallons of water quite adequate for doing the laundry.

In warm enough weather, I lug the clothes up a hill to hang on lines strung between Douglas firs. Sometimes that's a bit tricky, because the hill is steep and the grass is slippery. With a load of clothes in my basket or over my shoulder, I'm not super steady. I asked my running-coach son if he could get me some running spikes for hillside security. He thought logger's caulks would be better and found me some on Craigslist. They're a bit big, but grab hold like a dream. I end washday deliciously tired and proud of myself.

Someone said that it all sounded like a lot of work. I guess it is, and it takes time. If I were using modern technology to do my wash, I'd probably have sufficient time to drive to the gym and pay to work that hard.

16

A Little (More) Help from Our Friends

We are here to awaken from our illusion of separateness.
—THICH NHAT HANH

During our second winter in our half-built house, David finds a great deal on a Vermont Castings woodstove, a pretty little cast-iron heater designed to burn efficiently and with a minimum of pollution. I'm thrilled and want to install it immediately. But it sits there, decorative furniture—a conversation piece gathering dust, and cold dust at that—as the propane heater chugs valiantly on. Periodically I throw out a goal: let's try to get it in before the kids come visit, or before next winter, or to warm up the house for a party. Eventually we do begin and—big surprise—it's a bit more complicated than just hooking it up.

David (with occasional help from me, but more hassling than helping, I'm sorry to admit) glues HardieBacker ("non-combustible cement and sand, moisture and mold-resistant wall and floor backer board") beneath where the stove will go and screws it into the subflooring. Next we will tile the floor on top of the HardieBacker. We've never tiled before, but it can't be *that* hard.

Distressingly though, our first batch of mortar brings to mind the project of an inexperienced cook trying a new recipe, attempting to follow every inhale of the instructions without daring to put the brain in gear. The mortar is ridiculously stiff; the big electric mixer struggles to penetrate into dry material on the bottom of the old dishpan we're using to mix in. Dust flies, parched, while the mixer whirls and skips on top. Any good cook would know to add more liquid. But our measurements are precise. We do just what we read. As the "cook" of the moment, I read the directions again. And begin to freak.

"But that's what it says!" (Close to tears.)

"Now you stir for five minutes. No, the directions say you can't add water!"

We slap globs of too-thick mortar on the board and squish it down with tiles, most of which actually stick, though definitely a bit higher than ideal. Nine tiles are enough to cover the area immediately under the stove. Neither of us says so, but I think we both want to erase the whole miserable operation from our memory banks. For a while, I am even content to forget about the stove.

But after a few days, piece by piece, David begins buying flue parts: sections of black pipe for above the stove, the fitting and flange where the chimney exits the wall, double-walled shiny metal flue sections, and brackets for outside. And I get antsy again. "Okay," I say brightly, "Let's put two ladders side by side. I'll hand you pieces and you can screw them together."

So we haul out the ladders along with the first twenty-pound section of flue and—whoa!—I can hold it just fine but can barely lift it over to David on the next ladder. Once he takes it, I can't reach diagonally high enough to steady it for him. And as his ladder wobbles, he begins to look a little green around the gills. So I go down and hold his ladder, but not enough, I fear, to make the stretching and holding and installation secure. Finally he comes down too, with the piece of flue in his hands.

From the stove, the pipe must go four feet up, turn a right angle, go through the wall into what will be the greenhouse, then climb twenty-one feet into the air so that the top is above the plane of the house gable. That makes eighteen vertical feet above the roof gutter. How do we work on that? From a hovercraft? Sky hooks?

Then, *ta-dum ta-dum*, the orchestra music signals the approach of the cavalry. Up gallop Celina and Geoffrey on their white horses. Actually, they are in their 2001 gray Volvo, but the effect is the same. A strong young couple to save the day!

It takes the better part of a month, since they usually come out once a week, but section by section, the chimney rises. Finally it's time for the sky hooks. Celina borrows climbing gear from her dad: a harness, rope, and a Grigri, a metal belaying device with assisted braking. Geoff ties the rope on a porch beam on the north side of the house and tosses it over the roof gable, where it dangles down the south side. He steps into the harness and attaches the Grigri with the rope running through it. The Grigri's clutch will self-lock under a shock load—if Geoffrey should lean back or slip when the rope has slack—securing him in place. Then he tests it, teetering on the edge of the roof. And it holds.

Now it's Celina's turn to look green. A fine rock-climber in her own right, she can't bear to watch Geoffrey working high on that steep roof, so we trek down the hill to admire the chickens and the garden's winter weeds. When we return, the chimney stands proud and bright against the azure sky.

Suddenly, with no additional preamble, David and I are old hands at tiling. I mix mortar as if I know what I'm doing. It's thick enough. Not too thick. Smooth. David tiles the wall behind the stove and extends the floor tiles beyond the very amateurish-looking first nine. It takes us three sessions. Then comes the long-awaited last piece in the puzzle: David connects the inside black chimney to the great silver stack outside. I wish I could crack a ceremonial bottle of champagne over its hull.

And I want to build a fire *now*.

But we don't.

The next day I return home from an errand in town. I round the bend that leads to the house and look up to see beautiful, nearly clear smoke wafting from the chimney, above the roof, feeding the forest. What a delicious homecoming! I whip out my phone and text the news to Celina and Geoffrey.

During the next cold days we test David's air-circulation design. The second floor is open to the lower floor on the west end and at the stairs, and the downstairs ceiling has an eight-inch square opening directly above the woodstove to house a warm-air duct to the upstairs bedroom. Erika sent us a small fan powered by the movement of warm air. We set it on the stove and its blades fly, mixing and warming. We have no heat source upstairs, but the heat that rises through the openings warms the upstairs quite comfortably, and no heat pockets form near the stove.

We are surprised by how much money we immediately save. Not only do we no longer have to burn propane for heat, the woodstove also keeps my tea water warm and warms the dishwater. In just a few weeks we run out of wood, but fortunately, it is spring. Soon the sun will do the warming. Till then, we'll appreciate our sweaters.

When the logged south slope of our property was planted some thirty or forty years ago, the owners had in mind to grow Christmas trees, so for maximum production, they planted fir seedlings quite close together— sometimes as little as three feet apart. Then, rather than being pruned for Christmas trees, they were left to grow. And grow. Now we have many very tall, very skinny trees—not good for much other than firewood. Little by little we will thin them, making room for a few to grow well—and giving us a lifetime supply of fuel for our wonderful efficient little stove.

There's an old saying about wood heat warming you twice—once in the cutting and again in the burning. I intend for David and me both to get a chance at that double warming. Meanwhile, we need to build a woodshed to keep dry what we cut. No need to worry about boredom out here in the woods: there will always be an abundance of jobs to keep us entertained.

Along with doing his own artwork, our grandson Nate sets up display areas for museum shows in the hours between when one show is dismantled and the next is ready to be hung. They must be completed efficiently and on time. On a spring visit from Los Angeles, he looks at our exposed insulation and says, "I need to get a crew together. We could finish this in no time!"

As he has been either in Los Angeles or in Germany most of the time since high school graduation, we have rarely seen the adult Nate in action, but from his earliest childhood, we knew his perceptive intensity; as he helped us on landscape jobs during high school we appreciated his work ethic; and, as he leapt, balanced, and all-but-flew on roller blades in his early twenties, we admired his athletic ability. So we are somewhat prepared.

The next day, he has his crew. His dad (our son Jeff), Nate, and Geoffrey drive up with a pickup load of drywall. Jeff's purchase of all that drywall blows our minds, but we have watched him reaching out to others from the time he was very young. I'm thinking of three-year-old Jeff, feeling quite grown up, taking a sad and lost two-year-old by the hand and leading her to the nursery school sand table. In grade school, he helped his peers even when he got in trouble for it and would brave strange adults for his big sister when questions needed asking. Now he is a teacher and coach, has influenced hundreds of kids through the years, and is father to our admirable grandchildren, Nate and Celina.

Nate's crew tackles the tall west wall, which there is no way in hell David and I would ever have attempted. On vibrating ladders and balancing on blocking or the top of the upstairs balcony rail, they make like Spider-Men, juggling fifty-plus-pound sheets of drywall twenty feet above the floor. Young, agile, and fearless (none of which we are), they finish almost the entire wall as well as most of the stairwell in just a few hours. We shake our heads, dry our tears, don our monks' robes, and are grateful.

A mountain of construction debris taunts me from beside the drive. I pick at it: lumber with a possible future in small building projects in one pile; burnable wood in another; plywood and pressure-treated scraps in the trash, along with whatever bits of plastic and strapping got tossed on the mountain because it was there. I pick and fume. *Wouldn't it have been simpler to separate things from the get-go?* I work on the pile a few hours one day, a few hours the next, and the next week and the next month. *Why does the mountain not get smaller?*

One summer Celina and Geoffrey plan a celebration of their marriage, which had been performed quietly in a South Eugene High School English teacher's office nearly a year earlier. Their chosen venue is the meadow near the garden, just below our pond. I'm delighted, but I cast baleful eyes on that omnipresent pile. The week before the party, Geoffrey and his brother, Erik, arrive to tackle the mountain. By the end of the day it is reduced by 75 percent (why couldn't *I* do that?) and Erik has stacked burnable lumber pieces in a rectangular cuboid, creating a beautiful sculpture. A work of art.

The following day Jeff and Nate join Geoffrey and Erik. Soon the mountain is no more, and the whole group begins nailing redwood boards on the south side of the house. After a while, they adjourn to commence the wedding decorating.

On the last day of summer, long-time friends from my university days—Judi, Howie, and Stan—arrive with sander, nailing machine, biscuit cutter, a bag of elliptical wooden "biscuits," expertise in laying hardwood flooring, and enthusiasm for getting it done. I first met Stan when, as a student, I moved over from the arts and architecture building to the science building to take his fundamentals of ecology class. I had been frustrated that the landscape architecture department had no ecology courses (they do now). How can you manipulate the land, I wondered, if you don't understand the effects of that manipulation on the ecosystem? Later David and I sang madrigals with Stan and his wife, Joan, in a lovely group of a dozen or so, and later still, I worked with him when I ran the biology greenhouses at the university. I met Howie my first year working in the biology department, when I was assistant preparator in the general biology laboratories and he was a brand new professor, just fledged from Harvard. But I got much better acquainted when I team-taught with him after I began the greenhouse job, more than a decade later. I remember going to Howie and Judi's fifth wedding anniversary party, and now their son is thirty-one. Time flies!

David has assembled myrtlewood boards, stacking them in the order they should go down on the floor, with the board ends staggered and the wood's natural swirls of color placed together or carefully contrasted. The first row of boards must be aligned to accommodate edge tiling, still to be installed. Judi, the master of the biscuit cutter, goes to work wherever David had to make cuts to eliminate flaws from the ends of boards, necessarily cutting off the board's tongue or groove at the same time. Outside of dinner preparation, biscuit cutters are new to me, so I stare for the first few cuts. The biscuit cutter is about the size of a rectangular loaf of bread with a handle on top. Judi positions the board just so, frequently enlisting Stan's aid to hold it steady. She pushes the saw blade, which is mounted horizontally in one end of the machine, into the end of each board to be fit together, making crescent-shaped slots. David daubs glue and inserts a wooden biscuit into a waiting slot. *Tap tap tap*, we push the ends together, and *tap tap tap*, we ease each board against the last, rubber mallet rapping on a small block pressed against the board. We sweep and dust with every step, keeping tongues and grooves clean and clear, *tap-tapping* until cracks become only lines, smooth to the touch.

By the end of the day, it seems every end needs a biscuit, but Judi holds up and we get it done. Howie sands with ever-finer grades of paper; we sweep and dust, sweep and dust. Spent, but with the glow of camaraderie and a marathon day of work well completed, we load them up, hug our thanks, and wave them on their way. I'm thrilled to have a beautiful new piece of floor, gratified to have learned a new skill, and deeply humbled that people would so generously give us pieces of their lives.

This is how I know that our species can join forces and get things done. This is how I know the true meaning of *community*. This, I would even say, is why I think there is hope for our world. People can be so kind, so considerate, so giving. Insulation, a stove, drywall, hardwood floor. Dear family. Dear friends. Threads woven together; fingers interlaced. We'll get by.

17

Gardening

Oh thrice and four times happy those who plant cabbages.
——RABELAIS

I lie on the grass by the apple trees watching clouds float by. My back, hands, and shoulders ache, but it is a good hurt, earned at my favorite pastime: puttering in the garden.

Earlier, I arrived to dew-covered, fluffy, gray-green asparagus foliage sparkling silver in the low eastern sun. I stood and admired the garden—not only its vigor and promise of harvest, but its aesthetics—some of the things I considered in my garden-design past. I noticed texture and scale, shades of green and contrasting color, and inhaled the fragrance. Oh, fragrance! Oregano, rosemary, basil, thyme, tomato foliage. Their scent filled my lungs and brain till I thought I'd swoon or take flight.

I looked across soft-surfaced, deep-emerald, spade-shaped leaves in the rows of beans, their astonishing pink and fuchsia bi-colored flowers hanging on dark stems. Here and there young, slender black-purple fruits emerge. Close beside, tall, spiky, satin-green corn leaves reflected the light and caught shadows of other leaves moving across their faces. Beyond these, snatches of red stems glowed through immense, deep-green rhubarb foliage that dwarfed the bold, gray-green collard leaves nearby. Above and behind them, table grapes' medium-sized yellow-green leaves romp along our deer fence, their vigorous new growth waving in the wind. To the right, pole beans climb a fence, flaunting hot-pink flowers against green-gold foliage. We mowed down our ornamental garden, but this beauty is quite enough.

I squished aphids, thinking of Mother. "That's how you get a green thumb," she would say. I felt a bit guilty keeping the bugs from the birds, but our birds seem to prefer the strawberries. I weeded, applied fresh mulch, thinned new plantings, pruned the grapes, and planted seeds until I could work no longer. Then, breathing in the good air, I flopped down rather than trekking back up to the house to rest.

From here I can still admire the foliage, fruits, and flowers; smell the warm earth, the tomato leaves, the oregano; feel the sweet breeze playing with my hair, caressing my face. Later, if I am hungry, raspberries, strawberries, peas, beans, or kale will be much more seductive than would a peanut butter sandwich in the house. Or I can eat the weeds! So many are edible: sorrel, nipplewort, clover, dock, bittercress, miner's lettuce, chickweed, and many others. When at last I trudge up the hill with a basket of cucumbers, squash, beans, corn—having harvested the boon of what I've planted and tended—I feel like a queen.

My love affair with gardens began long ago. Most of my earliest memories involve someone working in the garden. I must have been very young—three-ish maybe, certainly no more than five—when my parents dug an enormous pit that I picture as a rectangle perhaps six by fifteen feet, and about six feet deep. I seriously doubt it was really that deep: I was a very little girl. But however deep it was, it was a Herculean effort. Then, it seemed to me, they threw in everything available—chunks of wood, broken dishes, anything worn out (this was in the days before plastic, so everything decomposed)—and refilled it, all an attempt, I learned years later, to sharpen the drainage for a perennial bed. But either it didn't work very well or they grew tired of perennials, as no perennial bed was there when I was older.

Even my earliest social memories are gardening related—though obliquely. When I was two and my big sister Nancy was in school, I accompanied my mother to the garden club. Mrs. Stedham's son Michael was two as well, and we got along famously. I'm sure the women appreciated not being interrupted as we played quietly on the back porch, making pies and cakes and other assorted goodies by smashing bananas and mixing them with wood chips. When Mother decided to check up on us, she questioned our resourcefulness, or perhaps the recipe, putting a sad end to our incipient gourmet careers.

But most of my early garden education was more direct. Each spring when the soil had drained enough that it would no longer slide and drip when squeezed, my family began to think about a vegetable garden. Then a plow turned the ground into a big brown ocean, with waves of clay calling me to go leaping from the crest of one to the next. I remember no crumbling soil as I jumped from wave to wave, so the clay content must have been high. Neither do I remember being scolded—though I may have had the good sense to avoid being caught.

I remember sitting under the red currant bush and stuffing handfuls of their tiny jeweled goodness into my mouth. And "helping" pick and shell peas, popping pods on the curved spot that just fits your thumb, trying to remember not to put the peas into the compost bucket, or the shells in the kettle. Now and then I would ever so carefully slice a pod along its back, so that I could fit tiny sticks cross-wise inside and sail my little pea-pod boats. I tell children that we didn't have iPods, we just had pea pods, and they were great fun.

Many of my memories of my grandfather took place in the garden as well. In summer he might push the cultivator, a wheeled tool with handles and a plow blade, between rows of corn to uproot weeds, or cut grass with his swoop-bladed, S-handled scythe. I would watch in awe, then hide between the corn rows and imagine.

I wasn't really supposed to play in the garden, and though I surfed on the plow's brown waves and hid in the corn patch, I obeyed that dictum in the ornamental areas. The garden of my childhood had rectangular rose beds arranged in rows, with a four-pointed, star-shaped bed featuring a tree rose in the middle. Surrounding the beds, climbing roses crawled on trellises. Daddy tended the roses, pruning, spraying, fertilizing, disbudding. Mother hybridized both species and miniature roses, grew out their seeds, and made arrangements with their flowers. Between them, my parents grew several hundred roses, entering them in shows from Seattle to Eugene, and bringing home piles of ribbons and trophies. They learned to judge rose shows, then trained other judges, eventually teaching and working as far away as New Zealand.

When I was nine, Daddy helped me make a little rose garden of my own and taught me to bud-graft, an amazing process that made me feel like some kind of wizard. You start by collecting scion wood—stems from the rose you want to increase—in February or March, while the leaf buds are still dormant, and storing the stems somewhere cool and dark. In June, when the sap runs actively enough that the bark will slip away from the stem of the growing plant you have chosen as stock, you slice a T-shaped cut just through the bark, on the outside of a stem, below the bottom leaf bud of the bush. Then with a sharp knife (Daddy had a special budding knife) you cut a dormant leaf bud (the small bump on the stem inside the petiole of an expanded leaf) from your scion wood, including a shield-shaped bit of bark around the bud. Next you carefully slip the shield under the flaps of the T-cut, leaving the bud itself exposed. Then you tie the bark firmly above and below the bud with a grafting rubber, and you wait. If you did it right—and you did, because your father was watching closely—the old and the new grew together, and a shoot grew from that new bud, bearing flowers of sunset colors, maybe, on a bush whose flowers used to be white.

I was also about nine when Mother showed me the globular seed capsules of hardy *Cyclamen*, each capsule a half-inch brown sphere on a spring-coiled stem. (The genus name is taken from the Greek word for "circle," alluding to the spirally twisted stem that pulls the mature seed capsule to the earth). With Mother's encouragement, I harvested the sticky, squarish seeds from where they had developed inside the capsule, planted them in baby-food cans with drain holes punched in their bottoms, and sold the seedlings with their pretty marbled foliage to the local supermarket. It might have awakened in me a bit of the entrepreneurial spirit—it certainly was a revelation that someone would pay money for something I had grown. I don't remember any particular delight in earning money, but I do remember the awe I felt looking at the capsules on their brown springs, and the thrill when the seed I poked into the soil actually made a little plant.

And that excites me still. The miracle of germination, the thrill of growth and bloom and fruit. And experimentation. Trying something new. Figuring out a better way. Or trying, anyway, even if it doesn't turn out to be better.

We garden on soil that would not be considered God's gift to gardeners. Rather than being rich valley soil, where fertility is increased as the river deposits its annual stores, this is land that spent most of its life under the ocean. Once the sea receded to expose Oregon, about 24 million years ago, this strip, which would become the lower reaches of the Coast Range, remained a plateau until the end of the Miocene and throughout the Pliocene, 7 to 1.8 million years ago, when the Coast Range mountains (along with the Grand Canyon, Hell's Canyon, and the shoulders above the Columbia River Gorge) uplifted. So here in the edges of the Coast Range foothills, we garden on old seamounts—mountains once submerged beneath the ocean—that have benefited only from the nutrients dropped from trees, from the decay of vegetation and other organisms, and from the deposits of erosion. Surprisingly to me, the soil is not rocky. The underlying mudstone flakes into tiny pieces when it is in the air above ground, becoming stone no more, just part of the clay. Those old seamounts are somewhere deep in the ground, but we've seen no sign other than the minerals in the clay soil. In order to increase fertility in the absence of a river's deposits, we add layer after layer of organic matter, which the soil seems to devour almost as fast as we apply it. But we keep dumping it on.

Our first raspberries grow and bear well, and they are delicious. Then they start dying. Raspberries are prone to blight and have a particularly hard time in clay soils that tend not to drain well. So one fall I decide to spread fertilizer and newspapers on a strip of grass about three feet wide by twenty feet long, then pile brush on it, from various of our prunings. After I heap up about a foot of brush, I haul compost to fill in the voids, and to cover it. The following spring, we plant new raspberries on our little berm. So far, they seem to be thriving, but I know from past experience that the berm will settle, and I must be diligent about adding regular organic material to keep those raspberry roots out of soggy soil.

Creatures add organic matter to the soil, as well as appreciating what we plant there more than I appreciate their help. Voles devour the roots of our strawberry plants, and my attempts to fight back seem only to encourage them. I read that castor oil does a good job of repelling voles and find it in a pelletized form. How handy! So, excited that I've finally discovered something that holds promise, I begin shaking pellets down the numerous holes. And hooray! It seems to be working. We find no new holes, and the plants look thriftier. We eagerly await the first fruits of the season. But when they come we think, *Huh! That's odd. Where is that well-known flavor?* Just too early in the season perhaps.

Or perhaps not.

"You are what you eat," said Adelle Davis in the sixties—along with many others before and since. And that goes for plants as well as people. These plants have been "eating" castor oil. Have you ever tasted castor oil-flavored strawberries? Yuck!

These strawberries are considered everbearing, which really means that they bear in late spring to early summer, then take time off, then bear again late summer and early fall. For the entire early season the berries taste wretched, good enough for birds and slugs apparently, but that's about all. By fall they are decent. The following year they are okay, but two years later they still don't taste as good as they used to. By now it may be another problem—some nutrient I once gave them that I've since forgotten, per-haps—but it also may be some long-lingering residue of castor oil. Some experiments turn out better than others do.

I have better luck reviving a sad corn patch. It is a long, cold, wet spring, and I keep delaying planting corn until I realize with chagrin that it is al-ready late June. Since we typically plant by the end of May, and always hope to have corn "knee high by the fourth of July," I know I am pushing my luck and don't feel justified investing in good seed. So I plant the end of a two-year-old packet that I'd not been super careful about storing. Maybe half of the seed germinates—a scattered, sparse, slow, and scraggly effort. The little corn patch becomes the butt of our jokes whenever we are in the garden. Perhaps one or two will mature, for all the good that will do. Then one day when I am carting the sawdust bucket from the bathroom down to the compost pile, I stop by the corn and wonder what would happen if I spread a bit around some of the wimpier plants. Not too close: I don't want to burn them. But on the other hand, I wouldn't lose much if I did, sad little things that they are.

In a week, those plants have caught up with their more ambitious brethren. I get brave, and spread my magic fertilizer around them all. They certainly don't make knee high by July 4—August 4, maybe—but I am still harvesting fat ears of delicious corn from six- and seven-foot plants in late October. *Vive le* pee pot!

Another experiment with mixed results was our venture into chicken raising. For years we were reluctant to get chickens because of the many predators in the area. We would need a good chicken house and, as we did not as yet have a good people house, we demurred. But in the summer of 2011, Jeff asks if we would like to keep the small flock (four hens) that had recently lived at the school garden. He had built a tight little four-by-four-foot henhouse inside a four-by-ten-foot A-frame, chicken-wire-enclosed yard. Together, the house and yard were portable with the help of a hand truck. He let the chickens forage and fertilize an area, then pushed the "chicken-tractor" to new pasture. That sounds secure enough to satisfy all of our concerns and, with the movable enclosure, seems workable in our space. Eager to become chicken farmers, we happily agree.

That September when school year begins, we're enjoying the chickens so much that Jeff decides to leave them with us, rather than taking them back to school. As the hens get fatter, I worry that they don't have enough room to run, so we wheel the chicken-tractor inside the fenced garden area where, with no young winter crops to be damaged, we can give the hens the run of that larger space in the daytime. Though they are initially inclined to hide under oversized collard plants come twilight, with a little bribing in the form of scratch—a mix of cracked corn and other grains—they soon learn to go back to their house when it's bedtime. As the Scratch Lady, now when I come down to the garden they run chirping to my side, rooting under my hands as I weed, looking for a handout. I try to explain that the world doesn't revolve around them and I have other things to do, but they (like most of us) clearly doubt that anything could possibly be more important than themselves. Eventually, though, they get bored and wander off in search of bugs and succulent weeds. I do my own weeding, enjoying the soft music of their chittering.

One evening we get home late from a party and run down the hill with our granddogs to tuck the chickies in. The dogs act edgy, sniffing the air, muzzling the ground. Then they sprint off, away from the garden. It's dark enough in the henhouse that I can barely make out their fat, feathered forms. They are on their roost, but acting almost as nervous as the dogs, perhaps because I woke them up. I peer up at them and count just three sets of feet. But probably I'm not seeing right, deep in the shadows. Or maybe one is back under the collards. I'll find her in the morning, I think, as I close up the house.

But when morning comes, we have just three hens. We search the garden and the nearby area outside the fence, but find nothing other than a few extra feathers under the roost. I think how agitated the animals seemed—both the dogs and the chickens—and feel sure some predator took advantage of our tardiness. With the help of a wildlife biologist friend, we decide the visitor was probably a bobcat. There was no carcass, so it was not an animal that would butcher and eat its prey on site. And it had to be agile enough to climb the six-foot garden fence or bordering trees to get in and strong enough to climb out carrying a fat chicken in its mouth.

We know that once a cat or other predator has found an accessible meal—particularly such a gourmet feast—it will return, so we are scrupulous about closing the chickens in before dark, and it pays off. We get through the next months with no unwelcome guests.

Then one sunny April afternoon I find just two hens, and some feathers in and below the fence. Broad daylight! I can't believe it. The cat has returned, and she must be a mama, desperate to feed a hungry litter, to dare a daylight raid. So we don't let our last two hens out at all. They will be safe in their tight A-frame yard inside the fenced garden.

Or so we think.

But I should know not to underestimate a mother feeding her young. David goes down early in the morning and finds two dead chickens, one in the little yard, one halfway out, stuck under the yard's bottom frame. This time the cat not only has scaled the garden fence, she dug under the 2x4 frame and into the enclosed yard to kill her prey. But getting the hen through her scrape was apparently not so easy as getting herself through.

She figures it out, though. When I get to the garden an hour or so later, only one dead chicken remains.

I sadly bury our last hen. I loved having those silly birds run to greet me, hunker down to let me pat them, and root around, singing, while I worked. The next day when I go down to work, the cat, if that indeed was the culprit, has returned, discovered where I buried the hen, dug her up, and taken her home.

For quite a while, I find other things to do, far from the garden.

It's too bad our bobcats don't seem to favor voles. It takes a few years, but finally, the voles win in the battle for root crops. Initially the harvest is good, but eventually the resident rodents discover our new offerings and invite all of their friends and relatives to the party. At first we have only a little damage—a bit of gnawing that would decrease storage qualities, but is easy enough to trim away. Eventually though, we pull up beets and carrots that are no more than a red or orange skullcap with a green feather on top. So I wave my white flag in surrender.

Surrender the territory, that is, but not the cause—it just has to be accomplished another way. We had our nursery for about twenty years—first growing assorted perennials, then specializing in native plants. When water problems forced us to move plants to the garden area in the lower part of the property, the work became much more difficult. Eventually I got tired of lugging plants up the hill and decided to close the nursery business. Left from the nursery are a number of fifteen-gallon pots—big, straight-sided pots, twenty-inches across—plus a nice pile of potting soil. The south side of our house, where a wall surrounds the area that will someday be a greenhouse, is a perfect place to grow vegetables in pots. In the summer of 2010 David places boards on concrete blocks in the excavated space. I round up twenty big pots and line them up on the benches. Many wheelbarrow loads later, I fill pots with soil carted from the pile near Easy Acres, sprinkle an organic fertilizer called "biofish" on each, grab a narrow-bladed trenching shovel, and stir it in. Our "pot garden" changes from year to year, but we now have carrots, beets, and potatoes in these giant pots, safe from the voles.

As late as 2012 that side of the house is still covered in white house-wrap, an incredible reflector for the southern sun, so heat-loving tomatoes, peppers, and eggplant in this pot garden think they're in Sacramento and grow like gangbusters. The first year we even plant pole beans in pots just for fun, which, growing to the top of the two-story house, look great but are not overly easy to harvest. We also enjoy having some herbs and salad greens near the house, where the greens are less handy to the rabbits, so we quickly fill all twenty big pots. Most of the plants do fantastically as long as we can keep the chipmunks from eating them when they are young.

Meanwhile I keep working on the soil in the main garden. The current fall-winter regimen for all non-bearing beds is to layer on spoiled straw that an unfortunate neighbor baled right before an early summer rainstorm, then sprinkle on some of my magic sawdust, cover with damp newspapers, and bury it all in leaves. When we still had the chickens, I also layered cloth row cover over the whole bed so the chickens wouldn't rip up the newspaper.

I put in the new season's garden in June, late as usual, and appreciate that winter cover. The adjoining bed is bare. I'll call it a controlled experiment rather than confessing I didn't finish the fall-mulching program. The covered bed is weed-free, and the soil yields easily to my hoe as I prepare rows. The "control" bed requires a mattock, and each blow jars my body and makes my ears ring. It reminds me of trying to garden a sidewalk. But seed by seed the little plants break through, and in a month or two, the "sidewalk" end of the garden looks no less thrifty than that in the end with the winter mulch.

The garden is my hobby, my exercise, my joy. The produce helps keep us healthy, and gardening without chemicals is gentle on the earth and her organisms. Organic matter added to the soil enlists the aid of arthropods and microorganisms to break it down, supplying a steady stream of nutrients to the soil and building a foundation for a balanced system. Conventional agriculture contributes a sizable percentage of greenhouse gases, according to the literature. Corporate methods often sterilize the soil, till it—breaking up the soil ecosystem—add petroleum-based fertilizers, and don't renew the soil with compost. As the soil becomes depleted, damaging insects and diseases proliferate. So chemicals are applied to kill the bugs and disease, killing the beneficials while they're at it. Like people who are dependent on pharmaceuticals, with pills prescribed for the side effects of other pills instead of relying on the healing power of their own bodies, these soils become dependent on the chemical cycle. Then the produce is shipped a couple thousand miles, losing freshness as it goes and adding that much more CO_2 to the atmosphere.

Organic homegrown produce, or that grown cooperatively or purchased from a local farmers' market, can be eaten fresh from the garden while still full of vitamins and minerals, and with the knowledge that it is free of chemical sprays. We benefit; the insects benefit; the soil and air benefit.

And so I continue this work that gives me pleasure, that helps sustain us, and that reminds me of my parents. I make up a song inspired by Joni Mitchell's "The Circle Game," remembering the predators of the hens as well as those of the plants, remembering the birds and insects that prey on the predators of plants, remembering that everything needs food and eventually becomes food. Season by season, year by year, successes and failures, delight and sadness, we're all together on this carousel of life.

18
Greening a Roof

The reward of a thing well done, is to have done it.
—RALPH WALDO EMERSON

A house necessarily usurps the ground beneath it from the green growing things and all of their companions, so when we began making plans to build, I proposed that we make a living roof as a way to return to nature the same square footage we would be taking. But David envisioned steep-pitched roofs, and we also wanted to collect rainwater. Neither of those ideas lent themselves to planting a rooftop garden. Eventually we came up with an alternative plan: we would run gutters from steep metal roofs to rainwater-collection cisterns, and would plant a garden on the ever-so-slightly-sloping roof of the root cellar.

But by mid-fall 2008, with the house half built, the cellar roof was still bare. So, quickly, before the rains would begin in earnest and we would lose Curtis, he glued rubber pool liner to the roof sheathing, using a smelly glue that couldn't possibly be good for his lungs. And then—oh my, have you heard this story before?—we were slow on researching how to proceed; we got sidetracked on other jobs; and we let it stay unplanted for a while—a long while.

When winter comes and the rain begins, several inches of water flood the root cellar. Since the land rises rather abruptly behind the house, water flow shouldn't be a surprise, but with my own hands and back I dug a deep drain around the house, laid drainpipe, and hauled in a foot and a half of gravel, so I am more than a little frustrated. David and I dig channels closer to the bank to catch the runoff before it has time to flow to the house's French drain, hoping to direct streams around the house and down the hill. But still, with each hard rain, the cellar lake rises.

Watching a downpour making puddles jump in the excavated area on the south side of the house where the greenhouse will be, it occurs to me that a big pit open to the skies is a natural bathtub. How can we expect the cellar floor or crawl space, all of them contiguous and at the same elevation, to stay dry in a rainstorm while we maintain this great collection chamber? The idea at least gives us hope.

But the seasons change, the rains stop, the root-cellar floor dries, and we relax. Then in midsummer I notice a wet rung on the ladder that leads to the cellar floor and think that someone must have spilled something. But it is wet the next day, and the next. Now a puddle appears on the floor. I can't reach the insulation in the ceiling, but I'm sure it didn't used to be that dark. It looks wet. *We can't have a leak!*

Curtis comes by. Balancing his dexterous body on wall blocking, he pulls down soggy batts.

I groan. We examine the roof but find no fissure—no possible place for water to enter. We scratch our heads and worry. And I head for the library, where I can access the Internet.

In arid countries, so I read, people for hundreds of years have built radiative collectors to recover water from atmospheric humidity. In northwest India, a school gets all of its daily water needs out of the air, from a rooftop condensing system. What is needed is a collection and condensing surface (such as a black rubber roof, perhaps?) preferably seven to ten feet above the ground. (The cellar roof is about twelve feet above the ground.) The surface heats in the daytime, and cools at night; the differential between the temperature of the roof and of the ground increases the condensation of the moist air. In the school in northwest India, radiative collecting systems incorporate pipes in order to use the water for the school or for irrigating plants. Alternatively, here outside of Eugene, Oregon, in the United States, the condensate can be used to soak insulation batts and drip on the floor. Very clever.

You'd think we could have predicted it. A black roof absorbing solar goodies, the cool cellar, all that insulation. But we didn't. So we remove insulation, improve the venting system, and swear to turn the roof green before another summer rolls around.

The many benefits of green roofs are more pertinent in urban than rural settings. In Vancouver, BC, the Fairmount Hotel's more than two thousand square feet of roof grew all the hotel's herbs, saving twenty-five to thirty thousand dollars a year, according to an article I read. A Toronto study showed nearly double the roof life for green roofs, attributed to temperature modulation. In the summer, dark roofs registered as high as 158 degrees Fahrenheit while a nearby green roof topped out at 77 degrees. Clearly, that difference in temperature also did much to reduce heating and cooling costs, as well as reducing the amount of insulation necessary in buildings with green roofs.

The climate quality of a town is directly related to the proportion of green space in the area, whether parks, gardens, or otherwise vegetated. Increased temperatures in cities—the urban heat-island effect—restricts air flow, concentrating particulates and increasing smog, causing a proportionate uptick in cases of asthma and other respiratory diseases. Green roofs can trap heavy metals, washing them into the soil where they are broken down. They also absorb sound, reduce noise pollution, help prevent fires, and, like any vegetation, reduce greenhouse gas emissions as they take up carbon dioxide in photosynthesis.

An important attribute in cities is a green roof's role in water management. On hard man-made surfaces, rainwater runs off through the drainage system to the river, taking along whatever oils, industrial chemicals, or other pollutants happen to be on the pavement, losing the benefit to vegetation and the aquifer of 75 percent of the rainfall. In Portland, where they had eleven-and-a-half acres of green roofs in mid-2010 and planned to green forty-nine acres by 2013, some roofs have had up to 60 percent water retention. That could make an enormous difference to the storm water system and cleanliness of the rivers if scaled up. On forested land, only 5 percent of rainfall runs off. In our case, the root cellar sits at the back corner of the house, near a cut bank that water will flow down. Even though the surrounding forest will absorb much of the rainfall, I will welcome having the roof garden soak up water that might otherwise run under the house.

Another benefit of a green roof is its potential to increase wildlife habitat and biodiversity. As cities get denser, less and less space remains for wild nature. Green roofs can provide homes, food, or cover for insects, spiders, birds, and native plants. Our root cellar is on the north side of the house, so it would be reasonable to assume its roof will be a shade garden. But in fact, it gets several hours of both morning and afternoon sun—at least in the summer. So I'll have to experiment to find what will grow best there.

As we already have the rubber sheet waterproofing the roof, the next step is to nail some of our 1x8 home-milled fir boards around the roof edges to hold the soil in. With the roof's slight slope, drain holes will be necessary on only the bottom edge. David drills two-inch diameter holes every eighteen inches along those boards, and I cut patches of screen-door fabric, stapling them over the holes so that as the soil drains, it won't wash away.

I retrieve the bottom half of the extension ladder from the root cellar, slip the top in its tracks, and set the ladder firmly against the cellar's south wall. From the rooftop, I receive the 1x8s that David has cut to length and now passes up to me. Then he joins me, and I hold pieces while he nails them together. Next we measure and cut black plastic on the driveway and I haul it up the ladder. I line the bed with the plastic to be sure that no roots will penetrate the waterproofing membrane, stapling it to the boards on three sides and tucking it under the front board. Then it's time to start packing scoria (aka cinders) up the ladder and dumping it on the roof for a two-inch deep drainage layer.

We choose scoria—lightweight volcanic rock—because we need always to consider the roof load. Rock and soil, especially wet soil, plus plants, could add enough weight that a poorly engineered roof could fail. The root cellar is carefully designed and built to be loaded, but we don't want to overdo. So we borrow Jeff's Toyota pickup and haul home a half-yard of scoria, and then take a second run for another half-yard, this time of pumice, both relatively lightweight as mineral products go.

My first bucketload of scoria weighs about forty pounds. As I struggle up the ladder, it is clear that if I'm going to move a half-yard of rock, it will have to be in smaller increments. Next I try a load weighing nearly thirty pounds, and must acknowledge that it, too, is too heavy for one-handed ladder climbing. What I can comfortably carry on the ground does not equate what I can bring up a ladder, my legs lifting my own weight, as well as that of the scoria, with each rung. I put a big plastic bag in my backpack and carry a load up that way. Much easier climbing, but a pain to fill and empty. So I go back to the bucket, shoveling in only three big scoops, for about twenty pounds total, that I carry the fifty feet from pile to ladder. I climb the ten rungs one-handed, with the bucket riding on the side of my leg or the ladder for extra support. Just before the top, I hoist the bucket onto the parapet with both hands, leaning my left shin into the ladder for stability. On one trip I bobble at the top, tipping backward, adrenaline rushing through my body. But I steady myself, set the bucket down, swing my legs over the garden rail and the top of the ladder and go to the far end of the roof to dump the load, which lands with a startling clatter.

After a few loads I realize that my right-handed hauling is not sustainable. Right shoulder, elbow, and hand, plus twisted back, hip, and legs—all are beginning to complain. So I alternate between left and right carrying. Then I try to equalize the stress to my legs and hips by remembering to climb with alternate feet, not right foot, drag the bucket, left foot joins right, lead with right again. In just a few loads the strain reduces. It's forty degrees outside, but very soon I shed wool hat, scarf, and vest.

About an hour and fifteen loads later, my body is still holding up, but my head is light and swirly and my eyes don't focus well. It's time for a break.

Then back to work. I get in the rhythm—three scoops in the bucket; bucket in the right hand; walk quickly twenty paces; up the ladder; sling the bucket to the edge; one more step up the ladder and toss legs over the edge; walk to the far side of the roof and dump the bucket—*crashity-bang!*—back down the ladder and repeat in the left hand. It becomes a kind of dance. And before long, after a total of about forty loads (approximately eight hundred pounds) the pile is gone. I rake the new drainage layer as smooth as possible and head inside and upstairs to lie belly-up on the exercise ball, giving myself a rolling back massage. I rub arnica gel on sore joints, pop a few homeopathic arnica tabs for my back, and look forward to a day off before continuing.

Next comes landscape fabric over the scoria to keep soil from sifting into the cracks between the rocks. I couldn't find any fabric that was wide enough, so must overlap three strips that are each three feet wide. Above the fabric we need about three inches of growing medium. One of the ingredients I'm using looks like small brown marbles, ranging in size from a quarter-inch diameter to about a half-inch. This is "hydroton"—little balls of expanded clay, used primarily for hydroponics. Nutrients will cling to their surfaces, slowly releasing them to the plants. I add the hydroton to the half yard of pumice and a bale of coconut coir, the fiber from inside the husk of a coconut, and commence another forty trips up the ladder. David helps and we become a machine: he loads a bucket and trades it for my emptied one, as I come down the ladder. White bucket goes in my left hand, black bucket in the right. We finish the hauling in less than half the time it took me to do the scoria, but I'm no less wiped out.

I want stepping-stones so I won't have to smash the planting medium and spreading plant roots when I maintain the garden, and we happen to have some thin tiles that were left from Jeff's kitchen remodel. Some are broken, and that's all the better, as their irregular shapes will look more at home in this casual little roof garden. So I lay them quickly, before my body gives out, then go inside the house to lie down again. Pain rushes through my quivering frame, as on the backs of a million little electric-charged snakes. But I feel that glow. Is this Cornel West's "labor that stirs the soul"? The glow is physical as well as emotional: if I could find such a chore on future alternate days, my thin bones would gain strength along with my muscles.

I take a few days off, but while I'm running errands or doing other chores, I can't stop thinking about what I want to plant on our little rooftop. This is the big experiment. As soon as my body lets me, I get back to it. I plant a few licorice ferns, which seem like a safe bet. They're epiphytes, growing naturally on branches of deciduous trees, so they shouldn't mind a shallow root run. And they grow both in shade and in filtered sun, which is what the roof will have. Our native sedums are likely candidates too. They should thrive in the thin well-drained soil, and they do grow in filtered shade. I tuck some shooting stars in a corner, a fringe cup and some columbine in back. I'll add some Oregon iris and native fescue plus whatever else I can find that might be appropriate. Some plants might not have enough sun. Some might need deeper or moister soil. I'll watch to see what does well and what doesn't and add or subtract as necessary. Topping the planting mix, and snuggled around the base of the plants, I add quarter-10 gravel, crushed basalt that has been washed to remove the fine particles.

The roof garden will change and grow. It's definitely in its infancy. But as newborns go, it doesn't look half bad. I'm excited to see what critters will chose to live there and delighted to have done so much of the work myself.

19

Inside the Root Cellar

To you the earth yields her fruit, and you shall not
want if you but know how to fill your hands.
—KAHLIL GIBRAN

Within the root cellar, now nicely insulated overhead with its new garden, we look to keep a winter's worth of fruits and vegetables. The moisture that has been such a concern still must be closely monitored. Most produce stores best in low temperatures and high humidity—but not in standing water. We used to leave beets, carrots, parsnips and turnips in the ground, just mulching over them in rare sub-twenty-five-degree weather. I even left potatoes in the ground until the winter rains began. But with our vole problem, if I need more vegetables than I can keep in our big pots, I buy the produce when it's in season at the farmers' market and store it in buckets of moist sand or sawdust in the root cellar. As our cellar is eleven feet in height, with its floor four feet below the floor level of the house, we have considerable variation in temperature, which we can exploit with shelving to provide for the different temperature needs of the produce.

Carrots, beets, parsnips, rutabagas, turnips, celery, and kohlrabi keep best between thirty-two and forty degrees, at 90 to 95 percent humidity. Potatoes, cabbage, apples, grapes, oranges, and pears like it equally cold but with humidity between eighty and ninety percent. Root crops keep well when layered in sand or sawdust and, in our cellar, require screening to protect them from mice, as, of course, does everything else. Cucumbers, sweet peppers, and ripe tomatoes also do best at about 85 or 90 percent humidity but need a bit more warmth, between forty and fifty degrees.

Our root cellar will probably never get cold enough for optimum storage for some of those items. The below-ground portion stays a fairly even temperature, around fifty degrees Fahrenheit, spring and fall, rising to sixty degrees when the ambient temperature hits eighty, and dropping to around forty degrees during the coldest part of the winter. That doesn't mean we can't store the produce that keeps better at colder temperatures, though; it just means they won't last as long as they would if the temperature were optimum.

Ventilation and keeping the ceiling cool with the roof garden should control excessive moisture in the summer. If the humidity should drop below seventy percent (which has never been a concern so far) I can sprinkle water on the gravel floor, moisten the sand or sawdust in storage bins or top produce bins with moistened newspapers or burlap.

Some things must be stored dry. Garlic, onions, dry hot peppers, pumpkins and winter squash, sweet potatoes, and green tomatoes all want a healthy room humidity of 60 to 70 percent. I keep them upstairs, sometimes in the lofts. Garlic and onions do best at cool temperatures, up to fifty degrees; squashes and similar prefer fifty to sixty degrees. I store my canned things on shelves in the root cellar, but so far, even on the wall next to the house, where it is warmer and dryer, the humidity necessary for the fresh produce is enough to rust the jar lids. Until I can come up with another spot, I'll have to keep a close eye on them, as excessive rusting can lift lids enough to break the seal and allow the food to spoil.

Food storage is an adventure and a challenge with its own reward. But it's also a competition. We are just two of the many local critters interested in a meal today, with a guarantee of more in the future. I plant in pots to foil the voles, fold tight screens over storage trays and buckets to keep out the mice. Now I have a new one to remember: I have time to harvest only a couple buckets of apples from the trees beside our vegetable garden before our 2012 trip to spend Thanksgiving with our daughter Erika and her family in Flagstaff, Arizona. But since no harsh weather is predicted for the time that we'll be gone, and since apples keep better cold and moist, I reason that the rest will last longer outside on the trees than if I pick them to store in the root cellar. It will be in the thirties and forties outside, much better than the cellar floor's fifty degrees. Also, if the apples were stored close together in boxes, the decrease in air circulation would let released methane gases speed their ripening. So I decide to leave what looks like as much as six boxes of apples on the trees, to be harvested when we return. It is the first really good year for these young trees, and I plan how many to dry, how much more applesauce to make, how much cider to squeeze and share, can fresh, or save for vinegar.

Fifteen days later, when we return home, I'm bushed. It takes me a while to get back to even remembering what needs doing, to say nothing of actually doing it. But in a few days I head down to the garden to see how everything is and to start picking apples. Our garden fence is made of chicken wire and fir posts, and as I approach, I see one post leaning badly. Fir rots fairly quickly in our wet climate, so even though I wasn't expecting it, I'm not too surprised at the lean. But I am startled to see one of the apple trees standing at a forty-five degree angle. We had heard that a couple of storms came through right before we got back home, but nobody told us the wind had been *that* strong. But in the same glance, I see a slashed-up jug of fish fertilizer and scattered piles of partially digested apple bits.

Now it's clear: we have been visited by a bear!

I left an orchard ladder in one of the Gala apple trees where I had been picking before our trip, and it looks as if the bear climbed the ladder and proceeded into the top of the tree, which responded like the baby bear's chair in the story of Goldilocks. Three main branches lie on the ground; half of the trunk is torn away; and most of the few remaining branches are broken. The rest of the trees are not nearly so beat up, though each shows some damage. A total of six or eight apples remain on high water shoots that I should have pruned off last year, beyond both the bear's reach and mine. That's all. So in my little lesson book I will note that you don't leave home at the end of November with the better part of the year's apple harvest still in the trees. And don't leave a ladder set up to tempt a thief.

On the other hand, the bear's got to eat too, although I wish it would acquire a taste for the neighbor cows that tromped all over our property while we were away, making deep hoof holes and splatting piles of metabolic waste in places—like the driveway—that don't really need fertilizing.

But we did get early apples as well as other produce put up in spite of the competition. Storing and preserving enough food to get through the lean months brings a wonderful, provident, independent feeling. Full cellar shelves give me more sense of security than a big bank balance would. And though they're sometimes pigs about it, I'm incredibly glad we have critters to share with. If I keep experimenting and learning from my mistakes, perhaps eventually I'll get to be as clever as some of the other animals.

20

Winter Food

Go to the ant, thou sluggard; consider her ways and be wise:
Which having no guide, overseer or ruler, Provideth her meat
in the summer, and gathereth her food in the harvest.
—PROVERBS 6:6-9

Healthy plants bear in such abundance that, not having a dozen ranch hands, there's no way David and I can keep up, just trying to eat their offerings as they mature. So in order to provide our own food year around, I research methods to preserve what we can't store fresh of that excess harvest.

My mother kept our pantry full of fruits, vegetables, juice, and mincemeat that she canned in a pressure cooker; in later years, she froze what she preferred not to can. I canned early in my marriage, then gave my pressure cooker away when our kids left home and I was spending long hours away at work. We don't have a freezer anymore, and as much electricity as one uses, don't plan to get one. I need to get creative with my food preservation.

When we were living in the tent by the pond, we discovered that our camp stove was quite adequate for water-bath canning. So I put up tomatoes, plums, and applesauce. Water-bath is fine for fruits, but for less acidic produce—beans, say—pressure-cooking is considered vital for safety. I didn't feel comfortable trying to maintain pressure on our camp stove and wasn't ready to invest in another cooker, anyway. But I knew people had preserved food long before pressure cookers were invented by drying, smoking, and doubtless by other methods I knew nothing about. Mother had dried green beans in a just-slightly-warm oven to take on our family's wonderful Packwood Lake backpack trip when I was a child, I remembered. I was fascinated, so started drying, though in my case, without an oven. All that is necessary in dehydrating produce is a source of dry warmth, good air circulation, and protection from whatever creatures might be about. You can buy or make a solar dryer, or simply lay produce on a rust-proof screen elevated a half inch, cover with cheese cloth or more screening to keep out flies, wasps and birds, and set it on the south side of your roof—if you happen to have a roof that's sufficiently accessible and not too steep, which we don't. Simplest of all is to put that same raised and lightly covered screen in the back window of the car on those days too hot to leave your dog there, or in the trunk of the car to avoid cooking produce in the sun. Green beans, thin-sliced apples, sliced eggplant (after it has been covered with coarse salt for a few hours to draw out the liquid)—all can be dried on strings hung in a warm attic or above a heater. After having let an almost-dry string of beans mold as the early fall weather cooled and the air gathered moisture, I am more cautious about assuring continuous dry warmth. A rack above the wood stove would be ideal.

When we still lived in town, I bought a five-shelf electric dryer that I now cart along with me when I visit or housesit at homes with electricity from the grid. Mice chewed holes in a couple of the plastic shelves, but the dryer still works. So one way or another, I dry tomatoes, peppers, strawberries, raspberries, apples, pears, beans, green peppers, plums, and more, while I continue looking for other techniques to preserve a bountiful harvest so that we shall avoid a hungry tomorrow.

Thumbing through *National Geographic* one day, I am stopped by the story of a preserved baby mammoth discovered in an Alaskan swamp, mired in a clay-like substance that apparently had suffocated and pickled her. This month-old baby was so well preserved that University of Michigan paleontologist Dan Fisher actually found mother's milk in her stomach, forty thousand years after she had fallen into the swamp.

Fisher had found evidence, as he was looking for ways hunter-gatherers might have kept large game for later consumption, that Ice-age hunters and paleo-Indians stored meat underwater. At one point he excavated an intact eleven-thousand-year-old mastodon. So he did his own experimentation, anchoring pieces of lamb and venison in the bottom of a shallow pond, and other pieces in a peat bog. He checked periodically for two years and found that the cold water plus the acidity from pond *lactobacillus* bacteria made the meat unpalatable to decomposition bacteria. Although its sour flavor and odor could at best be called an acquired taste, the meat was not only edible, it was nutritious.

Immediately after reading this, I find a book that helps me apply to my own life what I have been reading. *Preserving Food Without Freezing or Canning*, from the gardeners and farmers of Terre Vivante, an ecological research and education center in southeastern France, describes traditional methods of food preservation. The authors dismiss freezing and high-temperature canning, which they feel removes the life from food, in favor of more energy-efficient ways that are said to maintain or enhance food's nutrition. One of these methods is lactic fermentation—which is just what happened to Dr. Fisher's experimental animals, and apparently to the baby mammoth and mastodon as well.

I'm not ready to bury any animals in our pond for our eventual feasting, but I am eager to explore this very old, but new to me, preservation technique. I start with green beans.

When I was in grade school, in much the same way that kids now are shown scary films about sexually transmitted diseases, my teacher showed a film to convince us to cook our canned green beans to death, lest we die of botulism. Little Bacci Botulism, a line-drawing blob with an evil face, danced in the bubbles of the bean pot, chortling gleefully as the mom came to retrieve the kettle too soon. Now he would have his chance to multiply and infect the whole family. *Bwahahaha!* Unfortunately for Bacci, Mom got distracted, let the beans cook for their requisite twenty minutes, and it was Bacci and his family, rather than the human clan, who were sent to the Great Beyond. For all the years since then, I've been bombarded with the necessity to pressure cook beans, and to do it with great care. So I confess to a wee bit of anxiety as I nibble tiny bites from my first fermented beans. Is Bacci rubbing his hands in anticipated delight? I know this is a preservation method used for thousands of years. But do I know what those folks died of? Still, the beans taste good, at least to my palate. And the next day I'm still around to tell about it. As I eat them more regularly, and drink from their sour juice, I discover that my stomach feels better and my digestion improves. And I know I don't really have to worry about Bacci. As ice-age hunters learned many thousand years ago, acid environments are not welcoming to harmful bacteria.

Of course this is the same method used for centuries to make sauerkraut, so it shouldn't seem so remarkable. What truly is odd is that, other than in making sauerkraut, lactic fermentation as a preservation method had nearly died out, to be resurrected only quite recently. But it's not only good, and good for us, it's easy. No temperatures to maintain, no gallons of water to waste or scalding water to spill. And you can do just a jar at a time. No need to wait until you have enough to fill a canner.

There are a number of ways to proceed, but I simply pack beans into a jar, pour cooled brine (up to two tablespoons of salt per quart of water) over them, and close the jars. Fermentation takes a few weeks. Now, besides beans and cabbage, I do cucumbers, turnips, greens, carrots, grated zucchini, eggplant, green tomatoes and beets, and plan soon to try kimchi and miso. A great world of dairy ferments also awaits: buttermilk, cheeses, kefir. So far, I've not ventured beyond yogurt, but that's a regular: I make two quarts about every eight days.

I've enjoyed a breakfast of yogurt with fresh fruit and muesli nearly every morning for several decades, but used to think I needed an oven or special yogurt-maker to make my own yogurt. Another very illogical assumption. How did people long ago, or in villages far from modern utilities, do it? Certainly not in an electric yogurt-maker.

It turns out to be simplicity itself. All you really need is milk, starter, and a way to make and maintain warmth. After a recent trip to my doctor reveals higher cholesterol than ideal, I switch from dairy to soy, which is said to help lower cholesterol. So I heat two quarts of soy milk nearly to a boil, then let it cool to 110 degrees, tested by when I can hold the tip of my little finger in it to the count of ten. (Of course you *could* use a thermometer.) I stir up a couple of tablespoons of the last batch of yogurt for starter, and add it, along with about a half-cup of dry milk, to the warm soy milk, then pour it into warm quart jars. I wrap the jars in towels to incubate in a Styrofoam camp cooler, where I have also placed two peanut butter jars of hot water. The books say to give it eight to twelve hours to ferment. I let it go overnight and then move it to the root cellar.

Having called the process "simplicity itself," full disclosure requires the admission that I eat my failures. I read about a woman's first attempt that didn't turn out as she had hoped, so she threw it out. Not at my house. If the milk is too hot when you add the starter, the bacteria will die; if too cold, they won't multiply. While it's working, it mustn't be jiggled. More than once, my yogurt has curdled for reasons still mysterious to me, though I now think it has to do with either the milk or the starter being too old. Once I made a batch in town, put the cooler in the back of the car and carried it home, jiggle-jiggle-swishing over the bumpy pavement and around corners. That time it was like glue—which might have been from the wiggling, but also might have meant the milk or starter weren't fresh enough— and I couldn't look at it as I ate it. But I always do eat it, as long as it tastes good, even when it wouldn't win any appearance prizes. And as long as both milk and starter are reasonably fresh, once I invest in a thermometer, the product should hold up to public scrutiny.

One morning, as I'm eating my yogurt and muesli, I think of how much my mother enjoyed drinking a tall glass of buttermilk, clearly savoring long-ago memories as much as the drink itself. And then I remember my young self listening to Daddy explaining Little Miss Muffet's meal, which until then had been just words to me. He said that as a boy he had loved curds and whey, preferably with sugar and cinnamon. It made me shudder. *Lumps of sour milk floating in yellow liquid? Gross!* It hadn't occurred to me before that my parents' childhood diets would reflect their having had no refrigeration, while when I was a child, I thought sour milk was like any other spoiled thing—a failure and a waste. It is a gratifying closing of the circle that I am now learning what they of necessity grew up knowing.

Through history, the need to preserve food went hand in hand with the need for uncontaminated drink. Fermentation killed disease bacteria often present in water. Historical records from about nine thousand years ago show that people had already discovered that sugar-based solutions from fruit, roots, or grains ferment spontaneously when left in a warm place. The fermentation protects the solutions from spoilage. At the same time, it contributes probiotics to the digestive system that combat disease and provide enzymes that aid in extracting nutrients from food. It is said that the Roman empire's northward expansion stopped only when northerly climates were too cold for growing grapes for wine. During the colonial period in our own country, hard cider was the most popular beverage, its popularity dimmed only by the temperance movement that began in the 1800s, when righteous church-going farmers chopped down apple trees to save the mortal souls of family, friends, or selves.

So, focusing more on my stomach (and what I can learn) than I am worried about my soul, I tiptoe into the world of fermented drink. As a devotee of ginger brew, that seems like a good place to start. Fast fermentations, ginger beer and root beer among them, have low alcohol content—usually less than 2 percent—and are therefore considered acceptable even for children to drink; in fact, they often are much safer than water. I would have been smarter though, to have begun my brewing career in the summer. My "ginger bug," a starter made from water, sugar, and gingerroot, was slow to bubble in our cold house, taking more than a week instead of the day or two I had expected. Eventually, it seemed to be working. I filtered it; combined it with a boiled, cooled, and filtered combination of water, sugar, grated ginger root, and lemon juice to make a gallon; and poured it into a plastic jug. Then, wanting a warmer place for incubation, I put it in my granddaughter's closet, where she had baby chicks under a heat lamp. Early the next morning Celina awoke to strange sounds and got out of bed to see bulging sides on the jug. She moved it farther from the chicks and their lamp, lifted the cap to vent the gas, re-capped the jug, and returned to bed. At precisely 3:26 a.m.—*Kabloooie!* The ginger bomb blew sticky goo all over her shoes and the closet floor—but fortunately, missed the chickens.

Perhaps it was the long period it had taken to get the microorganisms working that did it. Or maybe in order to keep the alcohol content low, I should have cooled it right after bottling, in order to stop the fermentation. At any rate, I have a lot to learn. I've just begun exploring the myriad ways to preserve food. In time, if I learn well, I can grow all we need and have interesting extras to share—maybe even ginger brew. But next time, I'll experiment in my own closet.

Even if the time comes that I actually manage to preserve everything on my harvest list, I want still to be able to pick fresh vegetables through the winter months. Our benign climate usually cooperates. Some plants, of course, are tender and could never be grown outside of a heated greenhouse this far north. But I must consider their day-length requirements as well as their hardiness and take advantage of those hardy plants that respond to short days. Fall is a great time to grow spinach, for instance, which in short days will make lovely leaves, but when the days lengthen too much, will bolt, flowering instead of remaining in foliage.

I've known in theory about day-length requirements as long as I can remember but learned in a more practical way in the early 1970s, when I managed the green-plant division of a wholesale nursery. We wanted to jazz up our offerings and decided to plunge into the challenge of poinsettias, plants that require short days for bloom initiation. When growing a commercial seasonal crop, it is essential for it to flower at the precise time you can begin marketing. A late crop for holiday sales would lose tens of thousands of dollars, so we needed to control day-length carefully. We made frames around the greenhouse benches and hung dark cloth on them to exclude light. We raised the cloth in the daytime, and closed it before we went home in the evening, giving the plants controlled short days—or more accurately, long nights, because the length of uninterrupted darkness is what triggers the chemical changes that stimulate flowering. And *uninterrupted* is the operative word. We heard horrendous stories about crops that were delayed because of headlights passing by the greenhouse when the night shift went home, or even because a night watchman played his flashlight near the plants when he was checking the houses. But we did our research well; the dark cloth excluded errant light, including that of the moon, and our poinsettias came in beautifully, right on schedule.

I wasn't thinking about my greenhouse lessons, though, when admiring the stars one dark night shortly after we moved to the woods, I was surprised and confused to see a suffused orangeish glow on the northeast horizon. It looked much like the predawn light before sunrise, but not quite in the right part of the sky, and many hours early. After considerable puzzling, I realized it was coming from the city lights of Eugene, some twenty miles away. Thinking about the effects the light cycle has on the growth of plants, I wondered how losing a natural dark cycle might affect human health, sleep, metabolism, or moods, or how all of the other creatures and plants would be affected. I can't believe it doesn't make a difference.

I try to honor the natural needs of the plants that we grow, and fortunately for winter sustenance, many grow well when the nights are long. Beginning in early July, I sow hardy broccoli, cabbage, cauliflower, and kale for cold-weather harvest. I like to fill a few of the big pots by the house with extra-hardy carrots and beets too. Pots hold many fewer plants than does a good garden row, so I plant more frequently now. Early July is a great time to put in a second crop of snow and snap peas as well. I wait until late in the month for lettuce and spinach, when the days are shorter and, by the time the plants put on good growth, the weather will begin to cool. In August I load up on greens: cilantro, budding broccoli, spinach, endive, more lettuce, and, late in the month, arugula and mustards. Even September is not too late to start many of those greens. Some will winter as small plants to provide a pre-spring harvest; some I can harvest through the winter if I give them adequate winter protection. October and November are the classic times to plant garlic. Somehow I rarely get mine in until December, but I've always had good crops.

Most years I can continue harvesting kale, unprotected, throughout the winter—right up until the spring crop is ready. One recent winter I am bummed to watch the kale die after a few unusually harsh days, so I research ways to give the plants a few extra degrees of safe growing. Once we get our greenhouse built, it will be easy to extend the growing season on both ends, planting early and late under cover. When we had the nursery, we started seeds in both cold frames and "hot" beds, the heated beds being cold frames with manure supplying bottom heat under seed flats. For now we just make it simple: plastic hoops or other frames arch over rows or individual plants, and I cover them with spun nylon fabric or plastic sheeting or both. Then I must remember to uncover or vent them when it is not especially cold, and water them if they are covered in plastic—sometimes a hard thing to remember when it's pouring out.

But it's worth it. Summer's harvest put up and waiting, and more to munch direct from the garden, all winter long. It's luxury's lap, this home of ours.

21

Wildlife Habitat

You don't live in a world all alone. Your brothers are here too.
—ALBERT SCHWEITZER

One midsummer day on our morning walk, David and I round a bend in our winding road and come to an abrupt stop. Not ten feet from the road's edge, a huge bird, close to two feet long, stares at us with intense, wary eyes above its heavy, hooked bill. I've never before been so close to a red-tailed hawk, but its dark mottled back, white belly, and cinnamon tail feathers leave no doubt about its identity. We stand still as stones, trying to convey that we are not a threat. But eyeing us over its shoulder, the hawk hesitates only a moment, then stretches its wings to a good four feet across and attempts to lift off, gripping a rabbit tight in its talons. It wobbles once, twice—*uh-oh! rocky start, gonna crash*—and lands maybe fifteen feet away. There it seems to gather itself, shift its focus from us, and center its heavy load. It rises again flying low, barely over the tops of the tall grass, and drops once more some fifty or sixty yards ahead, this time safely out of our sight.

We talk about it all day, and many days thereafter.

How big do you think that red-tail was?

I had no idea a red-tail could carry a rabbit!

I wish we hadn't scared it.

Oh but weren't we lucky to come around the corner at that very minute?!

The hawk sighting gets me to thinking about one of our current projects. As we work toward defining and constructing our own home, we can't separate ourselves from our greater home. Not only do we want to consider how our use of soil, air, water, and energy affects the world, we want constantly to be aware of how the management of our land and our lives affects the lives of the creatures sharing this space with us. We recently enrolled in

Oregon's Wildlife Habitat Conservation and Management Program. This property abounds with a diversity of habitat with no help from us. Wrapping three sides of a foothill, it has north, east, and south exposures and a three-hundred-foot differential in elevation. Its types of shelter include the multiple layers of tall older trees—both evergreen and deciduous—smaller trees, shrubs, thickets, and open grassy places. A year-round pond and numerous temporary wet spots give not only ample drink for any visiting species, but habitat for invertebrates and amphibians whose life cycles include an aquatic phase. A variety of plants, both woody and herbaceous, provide fruit, flowers, nuts, and other seeds at different times of year for wildlife feasting. Food, water, shelter, a place to raise your young: the necessities for wildlife, as well as human, habitat.

My plans are mostly to accentuate the positive and eliminate the negative, as the old song goes, the negative being invasive exotic plants such as Armenian blackberry; Canadian thistle; our nemesis, the obnoxious *Lamiastrum* (yellow archangel is its common name, but arch-devil would be more appropriate); and if possible, the omnipresent herb Robert, *Geranium robertianum*, aka Stinky Bob. All of these, of course, I want to replace with native plants appropriate to the numerous habitats on the property. Then I look to improve the hydrology on this very hilly site, moving water more slowly, building intentional temporary ponds, dealing with gray water.

That's good talk, you may say, but haven't I been intending to get rid of the invasives for about twenty years now? What new magic do I have up my sleeve? And indeed, I do have some. Or at least have that intention. The magic is of the ungulate variety. I can't fence and train the deer, but I should be able to do just that with goats, and they love blackberries, or so I am told. But that of course will necessitate first building safe shelter for them. And even once we get a good goat barn, we may have a few plants outwit us.

Celina and Geoffrey's first home together, a shelter they built in our woods, was a "bender." They cut and trimmed pliable young fir boughs, stripped their bark, and bent them to frame a Conestoga wagon-like structure, binding the boughs with twine, and then covering the frame with white plastic tarping. Underground ducts from their barrel-stove warmed the gravel floor, making the interior space shorts-and-tank-top-cozy even in November. I threatened to move in with them!

The next year, when I found herb Robert seedlings on the *roof* of the bender, shot high from explosive seed capsules on this low-growing herb, I realized the battle of the invasive plants will be unwinnable unless I have lots of help. But I doubt that goats will eat either the mint-family *Lamiastrum* or the smelly little geranium, herb Robert.

Anyway, there may be more to providing habitat than accentuating the positive and eliminating the negative. Our morning meeting with the hawk and its breakfast brings up the complexity of relationships. Currently brush bunnies live in a blackberry patch on the hillside above the pond. The rabbits use the dense bramble thicket for cover, as do quail, various other birds, and probably many creatures I don't know about, so I need to remove the blackberries gradually and replace them with something doing the same job in a more manageable fashion. Wild roses are what I have in mind—our native Nootka rose, in particular—or black gooseberry. If we're careful about sequencing the blackberry removal, that should maintain shelter for the bunnies and their numerous neighbors. And I must remember that giving the rabbits homes is also providing food for the raptors, coyotes, bobcats, foxes, and more. Everybody doesn't eat nuts and berries, after all.

Sometimes we provide habitat quite inadvertently. Much as I loved growing the plants when we had our native-plant nursery, I was always behind. Part of the time I worked a second job along with doing the nursery. But even when I didn't, I never had the tidy operation that several of my nursery friends had.

One day I was cleaning up a neglected area and lifted a two-gallon pot that had been partly embedded in the soil. There I exposed an amazing sight: an enormous marbled salamander staring up at me. It was at least a foot long, shiny grayish-brown, patterned in black, with a large, blunt-nosed head and a tail flattened from side to side. This, I discovered later, was the Pacific giant salamander, *Dicamptodon tenebrosus*, the largest terrestrial salamander in North America, and one that is rarely seen by humans. As an adult, it usually hangs out underground in burrows or root channels in moist coniferous forests, or under rocks, or inside or under rotting logs. Breeding is near the water, where the female lays eggs in clutches of eighty or more, which she attaches to the undersides of partially submerged rocks or logs. Most unusually for an amphibian, she remains nearby for a month or two, guarding her eggs until they hatch.

Perhaps because the Pacific giant salamander hardly ever is face-to-face with a human, it tends not to try to escape when it is found—so I got a good chance to look at it. I found out from the literature that it can deliver a nasty bite and that it sometimes will head-butt and lash its tail to protect itself from predators. Also it is one of the only salamanders that can vocalize, making a croaking noise a bit like a dog's bark. But it was both quiet and apparently docile as I gazed at it. Excited by my discovery, I stared at its bulging eyes and admired its shiny leopard skin but then began to feel like an intruder and home-wrecker. So I replaced the pot—perhaps giving a clue as to at least one reason that I remain ineffectual in the cleanup department.

A few days later I did retrieve the pot and of course the salamander was gone, but it reminded me that although I needn't leave nursery pots lying around under the trees awaiting otherwise homeless creatures, I needn't strive for fastidious neatness either. I must always find places for logs, brush piles, and branches in my woods. It's unlikely I'll come upon any giant salamanders again, but I hope always to have a welcome home for one just in case—as well as for the multitude of other creatures I've yet to meet.

Some animals are just fellow inhabitants—neighbors, you might say. I'm grateful they are there and that I get an occasional glimpse, but I really have no hand in making their homes unless not destroying them counts. Once when I was walking in the woods, a pileated woodpecker landed in a tree right in front of me and uncharacteristically, I thought, made itself quite obvious, flying short sallies from the tree trunk and hopping about. After enjoying his show for a while, it occurred to me to search for what he was trying to distract me from. There, just a few trees to my right, a female was teaching her fledgling how to hunt bugs in a tree. She was nervous at my presence and eventually maneuvered her half-grown offspring around to the far side of the tree trunk, but I felt quite honored at having been party to the family gathering. And I will remember to leave standing tree snags and fallen logs to harbor insects to feed the woodpeckers.

Another day our granddog, Lupi, was being a good girl, heeling quietly beside me as we explored the hills beyond our property. Then, with *a growff!*, she bolted, and out from a ditch leapt a male black bear, maybe twenty feet from where I stood. I watched as the nearly black dog chased the bear, about the same color but almost quadruple the dog's size, down the hill, up the hill on the other side, across in front of a row of trees. I willed the bear to keep running forward and the dog to turn around and come back to me, and soon, it was so. I was never *really* frightened. Awed, yes. Anxious for Lupi, certainly. But wow! What a privilege to watch.

As we work on our own home and plan habitats for our fellow earthlings, we continue as well to make homes without planning them. Little alligator lizards multiply among our stacks of concrete blocks and lumber. I love watching them bask on the warm blocks, their long tails at least the length of their slender bodies. Tiny two-inch babies to adults of maybe eight inches, scaly, dark cross-bands over tannish bodies with black and white side spots identify them as they run up the concrete walls of the greenhouse foundation and disappear between boards. These guys eat ticks and snails as well as a variety of invertebrates, so they are more than welcome, as well as being fun to watch.

Some years ago a friend gave us a Copper Cricket solar water heater, which, it turned out, would have needed too much maintenance to be practical on our steep roof. Recently we moved it from where it had long been lying on timbers on the ground near the house, and in doing so, rousted a nest of brightly marked garter snakes, which I appreciate as they go about their slug patrol. So that is another habitat I'll continue to supply—though not under a Copper Cricket. I want to build a dry rock wall against the bank next to the east end of the house. The wall would frame an outdoor kitchen, back an earth oven, and give a home to lizards and snakes.

Woodrats make their multi-chambered castles without invitation in open sheds, in the cabs of derelict pickups, in abandoned trailers and, my sister tells me, even under the hoods of functioning trucks. I'll not make any special accommodations for them (they don't need special accommodations!) but I'll wait to reclaim the shed until the kids are out of the nest. Voles and mice also don't need an invitation—and won't get one from me. With any luck, the hawks and owls—and maybe even an occasional bobcat or coyote—will help keep the voles' numbers from exploding. I'm not crazy about co-habiting with mice either, but will continue to do so whether or not I want to, until we get the house tightened up or get a cat.

A garden shed is one of the things on our "someday" list. Because the garden is about a quarter-mile downhill from the house, I try to find places to store things on site, rather than hauling them up and down the hill. Fertilizers are in lidded plastic tubs; tools live in a container under a plastic sheet, and I fold row cover and bird netting, stacking it nearby when not in use. It's a lovely spring day when I retrieve some bird netting to protect newly germinated beans, and with a start, see a very large snake nestled down under the pile. For many years I wished we had a gopher snake to help us with our rodent population, and now my wish seems to be granted. Some years ago I saw a huge one when I was on a walk with our old springer spaniel, Sadie. It was at least five feet long and stretched across most of the road. Alarmed when Sadie and I suddenly approached, it shook its tail, trying to convince us it was a rattler. Sadie was spooked by so large a snake, rattler or no. The dark markings on its grayish body could be mistaken for a diamondback's colorings, but I wasn't fooled. I was delighted to see that we had gopher snakes in the area and hoped some might slither on down to our garden.

So finding this snake nesting under the black mesh is a welcome discovery. I am surprised though, as I move the piles of cloth, that the snake doesn't wriggle away. And then my pleasure and curiosity transform to horror as I realize this yard-long snake is thoroughly enmeshed in the half-inch squares of the tough, plastic bird netting.

Now what to do? My first thought is to call David for help, but he is up at the house and couldn't possibly hear me yell. I'm not about to abandon this poor snarled creature, and clearly, it can't get out on its own. Probably it was trying to get out that got it so entangled in the first place, in and out, through at least dozens of squares. Apparently it not only can puff up its body when it is alarmed, it can also shrink its diameter to get into small spaces. Where it isn't constricted, the body diameter is at least twice the size of the mesh squares. So if it is to get out, it is up to me.

In my bucket of tools I have a pair of scissors, so I begin at the end of the snake's tail, methodically snipping one strand at a time. Some are so tightly embedded in its flesh that I have to force a scissor blade against the snake's yielding body to get in position to cut. I talk to the snake. I apologize over and over. And I keep snipping, and snipping. My back aches and I feel tears welling. *What's that about?* I scold. This poor reptile has probably been half-strangled for months, and *you're* snuffling?

After about an hour of exacting and emotional work, I get to the last strand, holding the snake's head. One more snip, and it is free.

But it doesn't escape.

It never fought me as I held it and wrestled with its body against those steel-strong fibers. I was relieved that it didn't, of course, but worried. It appeared to be watching me as I worked and I felt that somehow it knew I was trying to rescue it. Still, I assumed that once the last strand was cut, the snake would disappear. I knew that it could go months without eating, especially during winter's cold, when it might have been in a dormant state. It would have needed water, but in winter that should have been available, even under all those layers. So why is it now so lethargic? Is it in shock? Does that even happen to snakes? Had it been too long without food or activity, or had it been too stressed? As I watch, it remains still, its girth now evening out and looking quite normal except for one sharp kink. If the snake survives its trauma, will a kink make swallowing prey impossible? I give it one last long look, apologize again, and invite it to stay in the garden if it can trust me. Then I trudge up to the house to fix dinner.

The next morning David heads down to water the garden before I'm up and sees the snake halfway out the gate, looking reasonably healthy, he tells me later, if not very frisky. He says that the body kink I feared would be permanent seemed to have straightened out.

I've not seen that snake again. I hope it's all right and I hope it's getting its fill of voles. As for me, I now know better than to stack bird netting on the ground.

Our most recent uninvited guests we will try very hard *not* to accommodate in the future. After we put redwood board and batten siding on about three quarters of the house, we went on to another job, leaving the remaining siding in a stack, waiting for us. And waiting.

In July 2012, Jeff, Nate, Geoffrey, and Erik set up their ladders and go to the pile to retrieve some boards in order to proceed with the job. Jeff asks for a whiskbroom, so I run out to check, not wanting the guys to have to clean off whatever detritus has accumulated on the boards and . . . *Oh my good goddess!* Thousands of big fat black carpenter ants! *Not* what I want siding my house. With a shudder, I toss aside the top board and it's a tenement, a whole project. Layer after packed layer. I get the big broom and start sweeping. The ants grab eggs and sprint wildly in all directions. I remember bombing scenes, the frantic villagers running, crying. *Our babies!*

Get a grip, woman, I think. *They're ants!*

They're ants. And I do appreciate that they have important roles as food for flickers as well as my pileated woodpecker family and other birds. I appreciate their own predation on other insects, and their role in breaking down wood as a first step to its decomposition and return to the soil. I would never destroy a nest in an old stump or log. I also know that as a species, they've been around more than a hundred times as long as my species has, and are likely to continue well after we've flunked our audition. I don't want to torture them. But I don't want them in my siding, either.

So this time we *remove* habitat. I sweep them up, board after board, and sprinkle a bit of borax on the boards so they won't return. I expect I killed a few. But most of them will find new homes and keep doing their jobs.

I've learned through both error and attention, to *think* habitat now: the fallen log, the leaning tree, the odd mud puddle, stacks and piles. Whether intentionally or inadvertently, everything we do or neglect to do affects someone—usually many someones. I could get obsessive about it. I don't want to be afraid to walk because of the tiny creatures I might crush, but I like being aware, and I hope to learn much more about all of my life companions. It's nice to know that if I ever get lonely here, I'm just not paying attention.

22

Foundation of the Food Chain

*I am myself and what is around me, and if
I do not save it, it shall not save me.*
—JOSÉ ORTEGA Y GASSET

Years ago, advocates for the environment discovered that though people had a hard time understanding whole-ecosystem concerns, they did care about many of the large animals, such as tigers or humpback whales or polar bears. So if the discussion was framed to protect the panda bear, for instance, or some other appealing animal, the conservationists were able to achieve greater environmental goals. Thus the focus has continued on large species that the public can respond to, in hopes that in protecting the conditions necessary for the charismatic animal, the whole ecosystem can be saved. Megafauna will wander through our woods and perhaps some will stay as long as the area around us is not clear-cut or developed. So for their sake as well as that of those considered less charismatic, I'm directing my attention further down the food chain.

Just as a stable house is dependent on a strong foundation, the foundation of an ecosystem depends on plants that harvest energy from the sun to power the rest of the living community and insects and other invertebrates who, along with microorganisms, are the 99 percent that recycle nutrients to make the whole system function. To best contribute to a functioning, healthy ecosystem, I want to focus on providing maximum diversity of plants and mini- and microfauna.

Because plants can't run from their predators, for many—I believe it's fair to say *most*—their primary defense is chemical. Some are unpalatable to browsers; some can change their chemistry to ward off attacking insects, to signal predator insects to come feast on the plant's enemies, even to communicate with other plants, "telling" them that danger is afoot and they need to call on their own defense systems. If we ingest these plants, the chemicals can be advantageous for our own health or nutrition, or they can make us sick. As I am trying to become more self-sufficient, I've been doing a lot of research about edible and medicinal wild plants. Frequently one source will call a plant toxic, while another says that it was part of the Native American diet. Sometimes this discrepancy has to do with differences in the chemical makeup during a particular season or the stage of growth or stress level when the plant was harvested. Frequently, the tests to determine toxicity were based on animal testing—perhaps cattle feeding in a monoculture, or experimental rats being force-fed—where an animal consumes great quantities of a single kind of plant, which they would not do in a natural situation. Many things become toxic in excess even when the constituent nutrients are beneficial in small quantities. Boron comes to mind—a necessary nutrient for plants and people alike, but an herbicide and a poison in large amounts. You could say the same thing about salt. Even raw green beans can be toxic in sufficient quantity, according to what I've read. The difference between food or medicine and poison is often the quantity ingested. I once watched deer with mangy coats nibbling on the very toxic *Aconitum*, or monkshood, a plant that is usually guaranteed deer-proof because it is so poisonous. I found no dead deer later, but coincidently or not, our deer soon had thick healthy-looking coats. Herbal cures, like pharmaceuticals, can be dangerous when overused, and few creatures will stay healthy with a diet restricted to one or two items.

So not only for the animals' health, but also for our own, I want to have maximum diversity in the plants. If the animals and we can nibble a bit from numerous nutrient sources, we will benefit from the banquet and maybe even self-medicate now and then, without having to fear overdosing on any one source. At the same time, more plant diversity will invite a more diverse fauna, and—most importantly—greater diversity makes ecosystems more stable.

I want to celebrate and augment the variety of plant communities already existing. I am particularly interested in improving our oak woodlands. Through development by humans and encroachment by Douglas firs, little remains of the oak savannah and woodland that characterized this area when the first European settlers arrived. Where oaks once covered almost a million acres, now less than 4 percent of that habitat remains, and associated species such as white-tailed deer, chipping sparrow, Lewis's woodpecker, and the wayside aster are endangered or lost. So we will continue releasing the oaks (by cutting nearby Doug firs, particularly those blocking the south sun), thinning small oaks that are too crowded for good health, and—once the goats have controlled blackberry understories—underplanting appropriate shrubs and herbaceous plants. Our mini-wetland invites augmentation too, and I can make a lifetime project out of tucking appropriate plants beside drainage ways, in shady woodlands, and on exposed banks.

For each microclimate and plant community, a different complement of invertebrates can find a home. Some of my earliest experiences with these creatures that wear their bones on the outside were from dipping in ponds and streams. There I found, among others, dragonfly larvae that looked far more dragon-like than in their graceful, brightly colored adult form, and stonefly larvae with two long antennae, two tails, and six segmented legs on the upper part of their bodies, reminding me of Kali or some other Hindu god or goddess with three sets of arms. Perhaps my favorite aquatic insect is the caddisfly larva, who wears a case that it builds out of whatever material is at hand: sand, bits of stone, plant materials. The first one I ever saw occasionally popped its head out of a diminutive log house made from fir needles as it moved, fortified and camouflaged, along a stream bottom.

A few years ago I was introduced to a remarkable dryland insect. On a field trip in the east side of the Cascades Mountains, the trip leader called us over to a sandy area in an open forest of ponderosa pines where a small pit—maybe six inches across and four inches deep—had been dug. "Watch," he said as he nudged an ant to the edge of the pit. The ant lost its footing, nearly fell, then tumbled down a mini-avalanche in the sliding sand. Almost quicker than we could see, *zap*, out came two sickle-like jaws from the bottom of the sand trap, and just like that, no more ant. The jaws belonged to the ferocious ant lion, a larval trapper. Our hearts beat triple time, as if we'd been to a horror movie that we had to see just one more time.

This mini-monster was the larva of the ant lion lacewing, an insect that in its adult form, with its long transparent wings, looks a lot like a damselfly. It is a cousin of the green lacewing, a commercially popular insect predator. When I ran the university greenhouses, I ordered several kinds of beneficial insects to keep our insect pests under control. I was particularly eager to receive the lacewings, reputed to be the most voracious of commercial predators. When I opened the box, it was empty save for some frass and tiny bits of bug remains. Apparently some early-hatching larvae had eaten the eggs of all of their future siblings, and then, each other. I appreciate lacewings in the wild but never tried again to order them from an insectary.

Through the years I have admired insects —their colors, their habits, or in the case of crickets, their incredible songs—and occasionally cursed them as they sucked and chewed my plants, but have paid less attention to their roles in the ecosystem. Bugs are not given much respect in our society. Think of our expressions:

Don't bug me!

I'll squish him like a bug!

They sent him to the bughouse.

But though they are largely unseen and unappreciated, without the invertebrates, life would come to a screeching stop. A full third of our food would disappear without insects to pollinate vegetable and fruit flowers; dead branches, twigs and fallen trees would accumulate in forests, providing tinder for fires while making the forest floor impassable for man or beast; birds would cease to exist with not only no fruit, seeds, or nuts to eat, because their flowers were not pollinated, but also no insects, themselves a critical component of birds' diets as well as that of many amphibians, reptiles, and mammals. Animal feces would accumulate instead of being recycled, at least for as long as the animals survived their own lack of food. And these examples represent a gross over-simplification, as each loss would trigger its own multiplicity of effects.

So we will strive for arthropod diversity. If we build it, they will come, as they will also if we don't mess with it. Infrequent mowing, little or no tilling, casual dead-heading, leaving occasional bare patches of earth, and importantly, avoiding pesticides—all maintain safety and provide shelter for a variety of bugs.

I am grateful that we have twenty-one acres, though more would be better. But perhaps it is large enough to be an island refuge from myriad toxic assaults. Currently, bees are dying from increased spraying of neonicotinoids. I have wondered how easily people low on the income ladder can live a "green" life, but the very fact of relative poverty can sometimes be an advantage. I recently heard that bees are doing substantially better in low-income areas because there, residents don't spend money on lawn sprays that kill bees.

Monarch butterfly populations, and undoubtedly other butterflies as well, are plummeting because Bt (*Bacillus thuringiensis*), a killer of caterpillars (butterfly and moth larvae), has been incorporated into the DNA of corn in order to kill corn earworm, the corn's lethal pollen then killing any butterfly that contacts it on the plant or blowing on the wind. (So remember when you eat genetically modified corn, you are not only eating pesticide, you are eating a butterfly killer.) Even more worrisome is the increased use of herbicide precipitated by genetically modified Roundup-resistant corn. The poisons are killing milkweed, the sole food of monarch caterpillars, further threatening the butterflies that were already in sharp decline from climate stresses.

Forests are routinely sprayed against insects and weeds, to the extent that local residents—both adults and young children—are finding alarming levels of insecticides in their urine. Perhaps the single most important thing individuals can do for the health of our natural environment is to avoid spraying.

Maximum habitat diversity should encourage a maximum variety of invertebrates: insects, spiders, millipedes, pillbugs, and others. With a good balance of bugs, the plant-eating ones will be held in check by the bug-eating ones, more pollinators will be available to pollinate diverse plants in several seasons, invertebrates that break down organic material to begin the decomposition process will help recycle nutrients, and the bug-eating birds, amphibians, reptiles, and mammals will have the best buffet.

We already have brush piles and garden mulch—both great habitat—and I hold off cutting down spent hollow-stemmed perennials until spring to provide overwintering sites for insects. Now I want to build some different retreats for the critters. Beetle banks—mounds about eighteen inches wide and a foot high, planted with native bunch grasses—make great homes for predaceous ground beetles, front guard for keeping plant-eating insects in check. Near our produce garden I want to plant a hedgerow, an informal hedge of trees, shrubs, and herbaceous plants that will provide food, cover, nesting, and overwintering sites for a wide variety of birds, insects, and small mammals, as well as invertebrates. The hedgerow should include herbaceous tubed flowers such as columbine, delphinium, fireweed, lupine, monkey flower, and checker mallow for hummingbirds and butterflies, along with similar hummer flowers on honeysuckle, flowering currant, and elderberry.

Since I want butterflies, I need to provide for all stages of their growth—their hungry larvae (caterpillars), who eat plant parts, usually leaves, as well as their better-loved adult form that float romantically about the garden sipping nectar. Some plants are essential hosts for particular caterpillars—like bleeding heart for *Claudius parnassius,* a beautiful milky-white butterfly with black markings, gray patches, and bright red spots that reminds me of a party dress I loved wearing as a toddler—and violets for the caterpillars of showy, black-marked, orange fritillary butterflies. But some caterpillars are more generalists. We have willow, ash, oak, and maple, all important host plants for butterflies such as swallowtails, hairstreaks, anglewings, and duskywings. In the hedgerow and the nearby hillside I plan to add yarrow, aster, carrot-family flowering plants such as biscuit root and desert parsley, and balsamroot for crescentspots, swallowtails, and others. And I will preserve our large patches of stinging nettles, important host plants for numerous butterflies, among them the lovely Milbert's tortoiseshell and satyr anglewing, as well as nutritious food or tea for us when the nettles are young and tender.

To complete the hedgerow, plants such as maple, sarvisberry, bittercherry, chokecherry, hawthorne, ninebark, ocean spray, Oregon grape, currant, and rose provide fruit and seeds for grouse, thrushes, waxwings, vireos, orioles, and grosbeaks; nectar for silvery blue, swallowtail, and other butterflies; and foliage for Lorquin's admiral butterfly larvae as well as resident deer.

In or near the garden I'll give special attention to pollinators, letting some of the cabbage family (kale, broccoli, collards, mustard) go to bloom. Bees love these, as well as the flowers of culinary herbs, like rosemary and oregano. This year I have planted buckwheat as a summer cover crop and a great addition for beneficial insects. Its abundant nectar attracts numerous pollinators; it supports predatory and parasitic insects that control crop pests, and its leaves are popular with leafcutter bees as nest material. One summer moment I counted five different kinds of bees and two kinds of butterflies busy in its flowers, while the nearby oregano was buzzing with dozens of honeybees.

Native bees tend to be active in cooler temperatures than imported European honeybees, enabling them to pollinate earlier in the spring and later in the fall as well as for more hours in a day. Of the four thousand bee species native to North America, 90 percent are solitary, rather than social, like honeybees, meaning they have no queen and no hive (and make no honey). A female emerges in early spring from her winter dormancy, searches out a nesting site, and goes about provisioning the nest. Some species use abandoned beetle burrows in snags or the hollow stems of trees such as elderberry. Others nest in the ground. She deposits a clump of nectar and pollen, lays an egg in it, seals the cell, often with mud, and repeats: food, egg, wall, food, egg, wall. She stores sperm in a special sac in her body, releasing it at will to control the sex of her offspring. She fertilizes the eggs to produce daughters; the unfertilized eggs become males.

Our best-known solitary bees are mason bees: shiny, dark blue, nonaggressive insects about two-thirds the size of a honeybee. They are excellent pollinators for fruit trees. Honeybees have been staying home in bed during some of our recent cold, wet springs, resulting in little pollination of our Bartlett pears. So this year, I plan to erect some mason bee boxes nearby. We plan to make these by drilling five-eighth-inch holes a half inch apart in an untreated eight-inch fir board, the deeper holes providing the bees better protection from disease and bird predation than did the 4x4s recommended in the past. I'll find a spot with morning sun and will make a little roof over each box to protect it from the rain, then hang it on a fence post. When we build our chicken-goat barn/garden-storage shed, that will be a good protected place to attach bee nests, but we'll need to build it within one hundred yards of the fruit trees, as mason bees have a much shorter flight range than do honeybees.

I want also to encourage our native bumblebees, many of which are already active in our garden. More than a dozen species of bumblebees pollinate plants in the Pacific Northwest. I was delighted to discover they might use abandoned vole runs for nests, which gopher snakes also might do, so I'll hold those as positive possibilities as I try to stem my ire at our plant-hungry voles. Bumblebees, social bees similar in community structure to honeybees, might also nest in rock walls or tree cavities.

I love watching the big fuzzy bumbles, their side pockets gold with pollen. They sometimes "buzz-pollinate"—disengaging their wings from the flight muscles, and using the muscles to shake their body "at a frequency close to high C." Collin Switzer, a Harvard graduate student doing research at the Arnold Arboretum, found that the frequency varied according to the flower being pollinated, the humidity, and the time of year, with the highest frequency being early in a humid summer. Buzz-pollination releases pollen from flowers such as tomatoes, peppers, and blueberries whose pollen is encased in tubes with tiny pores that open when the pollen is ripe. Honeybees are not able to buzz pollinate.

Many of our flowers attract bumblebees, but I want to be sure to keep the bees happy throughout their active season. Some that they favor include asters, chives, fireweed, huckleberry, roses, rosemary, and sedums. As they are usually both the earliest and the latest active bees, we need pollen early and late to keep them around. We have February-flowering willows by the pond. Willows are wind-pollinated, but their pollen still provides a good food source for the bees. I want to add more asters, along with goldenrod, to keep the bumbles well fueled in the fall.

I am eager to learn and do whatever I can to keep the widest number of insects happy, and to pay enough attention that I get acquainted with as many as possible, along with their endlessly fascinating interrelationships. Most wasps, for instance, are predators, though they also pollinate plants. We watched several devouring a dead vole, and a friend recently watched one stinging a honeybee to death in apparent preparation for consuming it. But they can become prey as well: David and I saw a big excavation, maybe eighteen inches wide and two feet deep, with four pockets near the top, where yellow jackets worked to rebuild what must have been a huge colony before a bear scooped it out, gobbling up stingers, hive, and all for a nutritious feast before winter's sleep.

Maybe more important than what we do to attract wildlife is what we refrain from doing. Experts recommend leaving areas of meadow unmowed, except maybe once a year. Currently we try not to mow between March 15 and July 15 so we won't disturb nesting birds. Mowing also endangers snakes and rodents as well as bugs. In truth, mowing or cleaning up most anything is likely to disturb someone who has made it his home if you're not in a lifeless environment. On the other hand, refraining from mowing lets woody plants, with blackberries in the lead, take over, resulting in the loss of both a meadow and its associated species, and refraining from cleaning things up is certain to disturb the resident *H. sapiens*. So we'll try to pay attention to timing and seasons, with the knowledge that when it comes to the wildlife, less is more, and we can always rationalize not getting things done.

Possibly more disruptive than mowing is people's typical treatment of the soil. Attempting to maintain or develop, folks pave, poison, compact, and till, often damaging or destroying the underground world on which the plants and animals we eat and admire depend. Arthropods and microorganisms make nutrients available to the plants. Fungal hyphae connect to plant roots, providing the plants with water and nutrients from afar. Along with roots of plants, fungal mycelial mats hold on to soil, keeping it from washing away. Fungal mycelium cleans pollutants from the ground before they can be carried to waterways. (One of my plans is to fill a swale beside a new chicken yard near our house with fungi-inoculated bark, to filter out bacteria that would otherwise run from the yard, down the hill to our pond.) Fungi can even help plants communicate in emergencies, as scientists have discovered. Probably more goes on in that subterranean world than even the scientists who study it know, but enough is known to tell us to treat it with respect.

I find insects in odd places. As I put drops in David's eyes to ward off glaucoma, I find an apple-green katydid nestled in his curly gray beard. That probably wouldn't be considered a sustainable habitat, but it is a lovely color combination and gives me a super idea for painting the walls in the great room.

23
Happiness

No man is happy who does not think himself so.

Practice is the best of all instructors.
— PUBLILIUS SYRUS

I sit on the main floor of our growing nest, wondering if it will ever be completed; wondering if, as we get deeper into our golden years, we'll have the muscle power and energy to keep building; wondering if it even really matters. Truth to tell, life is pretty good just as it is. Friends refer to my "dream house" and they're happy for me. But in my house and my greater home in the world, even a perfect design perfectly executed wouldn't necessarily make me happy if I weren't so inclined. I could always find some irritation or lack, something to be annoyed about or want.

I remember a placard I saw in front of one of our old favorite watering holes, its blue balloon letters with scarlet ghosts proclaiming "Attitude Adjustment Hour 4–6 p.m. Drinks 20% Off." Images flit through my mind: Frowny Face enters and emerges as Smiley Face. Smiley Face enters and emerges with blackened eyes and blood dripping from the now down-turned mouth. A suit stalks in, collar open, tie askew, brow corrugated in horizontal plowlines. He knocks back three glasses in rushed silence, then the oral spigot opens and the muttering begins. His effing sonabitch boss effing wouldn't know a good idea if it gawdam effed him in the rear. One day he's going to tell the sonabitch where to shove his effing job. And on and expletive-deleted on. Two more hours of attitude adjustment and he reels out the door and careens toward home, where he will dutifully prepare for another effing day.

Attitude adjustment. It's not what happens that counts, it's how you react to it, or so they say. The year before I graduated from high school,

Norman Vincent Peale's newly published *The Power of Positive Thinking* was praised by some as the path to self-confidence and deliverance from suffering while others called it self-hypnosis and wishful thinking, or even a dangerous precursor to disillusionment and mental illness. Peale's philosophy was of the "smile and the world smiles with you" variety and some feared the effects of all that smiling.

Yet I think back to myself at about age seven or eight, fulfilling my patriotic duty as I saw it by waving and smiling at the young men in each and every army jeep caravanning for miles down Highway 99, troops on their way to the base where they would ship out for action in World War II. My cheeks ached, but I couldn't allow them to relax. The last jeep in the caravan deserved as good a send-off as the first. Chances are that the earnest, smiling little girl did distract some of the soldiers, at least briefly, from thoughts of the war they were about to join. I remember some returned waves and smiles. I had no real concept of what they would be facing, of course, but I went home feeling that I had worked hard for an important cause. Smile, and a small part of the world will probably smile back, even if just for a moment.

Seventeen muscles are necessary for a person to smile. I gave all seventeen a good workout, and they told me about it. But we work *forty-three* muscles to make a frown. So do we frown because we feel stress, I wonder, or feel stress because we are frowning? According to an article I read, smiling releases endorphins, natural painkillers, and serotonin—a real cocktail of feel-good drugs. A bit like happy hour, but without the hangover.

One of Norman Vincent Peale's critics said that his positive talk would "drum out the inner voice that is the spur to inner growth." I would hope that it was possible for me to start the day with a smile—with gratitude for life and love and the good earth—and still to ask all of my inner voices to step forward and reveal their agendas, as an advice columnist put it. I'm trying to learn to listen to those voices in a non-judgmental way. I'd like to think that if I am attentive to what's going on inside, I can make my own attitude adjustment. If I can't see that the glass is half empty, how would I know to get the pitcher to fill it up? But I needn't cry, need I, unless I choose to fill it with my tears? And maybe filling it just might inspire a smile.

Here in America we consider it our inalienable right to pursue happiness. Pursuing, chasing, striving for something we don't have. We look for it in alcohol, in drugs, in stores. It's what our economy is based on. Perhaps it is also why our citizens use so many anti-depressants.

On a radio program, an environmental scientist pointed out that it is the Western desire to acquire—the idea that getting more stuff will make us happy—that is depleting resources, devastating numerous species, destroying the environment, and causing climate change. An economist countered that without that desire, our economy would collapse. No one suggested changing the basis of the economy, or pointed out that the current basis was failing miserably at making people happy. Nor did they mention that even a great economy wouldn't do us much good without an environment we can live in.

Trolling the malls for happiness isn't my idea of the good life. It's understandable to pursue pleasure, fleeting though it often is, but happiness is an attitude—a decision. You might wonder how—in the face of wars, poverty, famine, and climate craziness—one can be happy, but I would ask, what good is accomplished by being otherwise? And I do feel happy as I sit here on the main floor of our house, its foundation and my ancestors firmly supporting me, and think about how I intend to live within—and beyond—its walls. Building a house is just making a structure. It takes much more to make a home.

We know some folks—I hesitate to call them a couple—who built a beautiful house in a storybook wooded setting. They lived in opposite wings, and last I knew, hadn't spoken to each other in a decade. I wonder what their original intentions were. Others choose holy acrimony or mutual hurt feelings. I give credit to our son and his former wife, who were wise enough to recognize that their individual ideas of making a home would never mesh. An oriole and an osprey, evolved for different nests and different lives, their clear-eyed response was to take separate paths to discover their unique intentions. What point is there to spending one's brief life occupying opposite wings in a house of discontent? And yet . . .

And yet, I would want to make sure the discontent did not live within myself. Would I know how to find happiness in that mythical "next time"?

One of my perennial frustrations is not discontent with others or with my circumstances, but with myself. Making a home may entail a certain transformation of the self. Too often, I do not measure up to my intentions.

Intend. From the Old French *entendre* and Latin *intendere*, to stretch out for, to aim for.

I *intend* to live lightly, to take sparingly from nature's gifts, to return or augment as much as possible. But for a week I housesit in town and with a shock realize that I am letting the water run as I wash the carrots or my hands, that I am flipping the light switch on as I enter a room, even though it is 2:00 o'clock on a clear fall afternoon—flipping it, I suppose, because it is there. I look around furtively, feeling like an alcoholic newly fallen from the wagon. Who is watching?

How can this be? For twenty years I have lived without running water or electricity in my house, and after the initial struggles to get over old habits, I not only appreciated merits in my new way of living, I found it not at all difficult. Now so quickly I fall into old ways. Are the sirens of convenience that seductive?

And I'm afraid the answer is yes. At least I can't resist without a lot of thought and attention. I have even crashed into doors in public buildings, because I expected them to open for me. But my current way of life is not something I'm just enduring. It is something I am committed to, and something that brings me joy.

As long as we live in the woods, much of our chosen lifestyle takes care of itself. Our solar panels charge only when the sun shines. At night when we draw electricity from the batteries the sun has filled during the day, we can watch the trimetric—the meter on the wall that tells us how full the batteries are and how much we are using —2.4 amps for the kitchen lights, 1.5 for the radio, 2.7 for the mudroom lights, 3.8 for the coffee grinder, 75 amps (wow! I sure won't use that for very long at a time) for the vacuum. Each day when the sun is out I charge the computer, which takes 2 amps, including the demands of the power strip, and each evening, I empty it in about two and a half hours, then turn the inverter back on. If the solar batteries get dangerously low—much below 24.6 volts—we simply turn everything off and wait for tomorrow's sun to recharge them again. Water use too, is easy to monitor. We carry well water from a pipe near the house, filling a six-gallon carboy. This makes it clear how much we use and when we must refill it.

So the solution, I guess, is that I must police myself. When (if?) our pipes get hooked up here, or if I must at some point live in town, I need to find a way to continue to live the way I want to live. Some years ago I had a discussion—an argument, probably—with my friend Jake about the relative water economy of showers versus baths. He contended that much less water was used in a shower. That was inconceivable to me. Baths clearly took less. Eventually we realized that he was thinking of long-ago army showers: get wet quickly under a brief splash, turn the water off and suds up, turn back on to rinse, and you're done. I was remembering childhood baths in an inch of water, versus long luxurious showers. So with a little discipline, I can use water Jake's way: wet the carrot (or my hands or toothbrush or body), turn the water off and scrub, water back on to rinse, and off again.

Without discipline, I'll have to make it easy for myself. If I were serious about pursuing a diet, would I surround myself with open bowls of chocolates, cookies, and chips, with a freezer full of ice cream? If I were a recovering alcoholic, would I hang out at a wine tasting? Perhaps the trick is to continue using water from a container whose capacity I know, and be sure always to have a meter to measure my energy use.

I *intend* also to stay physically fit so that I can continue to live an active life. In my forties and early fifties I ran regularly, competing in road runs from 10Ks to marathons as well as middle distances on the track. During that period I learned about weight lifting and gloried in the new muscles in my upper arms. In my mid-fifties I began gardening professionally and found more muscles I hadn't known about. In my early sixties I did a bit too much, felt broken down and over the hill. (*It's gone, all gone, poor me.*) So I got a gym membership, discovered circuit training, and welcomed a renewed body. More years passed. I fell a lot. My balance left. (*Ol' rockin' chair's got me, alas.*) A few weeks of physical therapy and I was standing solidly on one foot, heron-like. Not spearing fish with my bill, but maybe soon.

I *intend* to write. I sit down faithfully from two to four hours every evening, and I think about that writing throughout the day. When I walk, when I garden, my muse is with me. I dream ideas, turns of phrase. Then I get sidetracked in meetings, social occasions, appointments, commitments. I don't write for weeks. Do I even remember what I was trying to say? Or how to say it?

I *intend* to be responsible for my emotions. I finally learned not to take personally other people's behavior. If she doesn't speak to me, she probably has something else on her mind, rather than purposely snubbing me. If he is grouchy, chances are he's not feeling great. Most likely I didn't cause it. Fact is I'm not that bloody important. It's like the middle-school girl dying inside, mortified because everyone will notice that her hair ribbon is the wrong color and think she's a real dork, when of course everyone is worried about what everybody else is thinking of *them*, not looking at her at all.

During a counseling session, when the distraught woman said, "He makes me so angry!" the guru replied, "He *makes* you angry? How can he *make* you angry? Are you his slave? You *choose* to react in anger."

The corollary to my not being someone else's slave is that no one is my slave either. If I make a honey-do list and honey doesn't, it is not a personal assault. *Strawberry plant, if you really loved me, you would bear chocolate-covered fruits on my special day. If you really cared.* But if that chocolate covering is so important, maybe I should find a way to dip my own damn strawberry. My friend might not agree that we became roommates in order for me to have someone to fulfill my personal dreams and fantasies. Maybe all close business or personal relationships should be preceded by an obligatory mission statement from each party involved. Then we would see what was important to the other person, how and by whom it was to be accomplished, and whether that was a game we really wanted to play.

I accepted intellectually that I shouldn't take things personally before my gut accepted it. Somewhere in my life I picked up a pretty good load of guilt, something I can blame no one for but myself. It was hard to get rid of even after I realized the arrogance of it. Really, I don't make the world go round. But one day I did make that shift, from understanding as fact to feeling and believing deep down.

David gets tense as we prepare to go places. He explains it as a carryover from his early years living across the water from Seattle, where ferry schedules were not flexible. If you were late to the ferry, you were left behind. So on the way to the car this day, he snapped at me about something and I reacted in the old familiar wounded way. But this time, I became as two people—a divided consciousness. I watched myself reacting, was aware of the feelings and the illogic of them, and they dissolved. That was the beginning of a whole new way to respond. *What's that lump in my gut about? When/why did my throat start to tighten? What can I do about it?*

When dear friends offered not only to help install some flooring but also to purchase the myrtlewood, wouldn't you have expected me to feel overwhelmed with relief and gratitude? I was overwhelmed, yes, but it was as if a volcano was erupting inside of me. My head got light, my legs were wobbly, my heart thumped double-time, and tears welled. So what was *that* all about? Some sort of false pride? Was it the two-year-old's *me can do it meself*? (So if me can, why does me not?) Or maybe *I* should *do it myself*? (Well, perhaps. But let's live in the real world!) Then I caught my alter ego from somewhere deep inside me, singing that sad old hymn that begins *I am not worthy. I am not worthy* . . . Good grief! I don't even believe in that. I don't think any of us is worthy or unworthy. We just are. I feel blessed for all of the gifts of life, but I neither feel that I am owed them or that I *don't* deserve them. The fact is, I'd love to do something similar for someone else if I could. I discovered that joy when I was very young.

Six or seven years old, I had missed the bus and was frantically running the two miles to school. If I was late, I'd have to go to the principal's office, and if I got in trouble at school, surely I would get in trouble at home as well. My focus was straight ahead, desperate, miserable. Maybe halfway there, I heard a little girl crying. Her wagon was turned over and she couldn't get it back on its wheels. I stopped abruptly, flipped it over for her, and turned to go. Her crying ceased as if a switch had been thrown and she stared at me in astonishment. Suddenly my feet had wings. I sailed happily into class before the bell rang and felt buoyed up all day. That little girl may have been happy that her wagon was now upright—I hope so. But she couldn't have been as happy as I was. And I'll never forget that astounding revelation.

I do believe in community. And community goes both ways—or a whole network of ways, actually, as do the communities of nature. We give what we can and we receive gratefully. So, crazy reactions can also give insights into subconscious selves. If I stay aware of the physiological cues, I can not only learn a bit about myself, I can switch off the emotional trigger before it grabs hold of me. But I have to practice.

I have to practice. Each of these things—living lightly, staying fit, writing with discipline, managing emotions—I care about, and I have failed at each to a greater or lesser degree and more or less often. Each time, I am frustrated, confused. (I *care*! I *know* better! What's *wrong* with me?) Now

I'm trying to look at a situation and understand its cause without assigning guilt or blame. *This is what it is. Where do we go from here?*

But I have to keep working at it. I'm learning that, finally. I can't take one drink of water and assuage my thirst forever. I can't buy an exercise machine and get fit unless I use it. If I want to be a mountain climber, I must climb mountains, not just read *National Geographic*. If I want to eat nutritionally, that's a full-time deal, not just a good meal now and then. Whether it's living lightly or staying in shape or developing empathy or evicting negative emotions, it takes work. There's a reason Buddhists call their daily meditation their "practice." It's not enough to lean toward a goal; I must keep at it. I must faithfully attend to my intentions.

At yoga today, with one foot placed firmly against the inside of the opposite calf and both arms stretching into the air, I became a tree. Not as well rooted as most trees certainly, but doing a good job of shaking my leaves in the breeze, along with most every other cell in my body. When I had my landscaping business, I learned that if you stake young trees too tightly, they cannot move in the wind, and they grow thin and weak. It is the movement—blowing with and resistance to the wind—that stimulates the cell growth that makes trunks sturdy. At the time I wondered if, like the restricted sapling, the emotional or intellectual growth of a tightly regimented child would be inhibited, compared to a child who has a chance to shake in the wind—to explore, to make some of her own choices and learn from her mistakes. But now I think the analogy could be far broader.

As I stand in my yoga class, wobbling on one foot, trying to find balance, I also strive to break bad habits and form good ones, teetering, settling in, floundering again. So, too, are relationships a dance—whirling, dipping, stumbling, coming together, turning away, seeking balance. The ecosystem strives to balance its energy and its producing, consuming, decomposing crew. The coming together, the goal successfully met, the healthy ecosystem, each is a reward and a thrill at least partly because we measure it against the wobble. But true balance is a static state. Planets we have observed in space are in equilibrium. They are static: dead. It is the imbalance that drives function in the biosphere, in the relationship, in the individual. Yet too far *out* of balance, a person's physical or mental health is endangered; friends and nations battle; marriages dissolve; species die;

ecosystems turn barren; the living tree and the yoga practitioner fall. Life is in the trying.

And that makes me happy. Working at something important to me. Seeing small successes. Understanding the failures. Trying again. Tuning in to the emotions of others and recognizing them in myself.

Accepting gifts gratefully.

Helping when I can.

Paying attention.

Making a home.

Making a life.

24
New Model

We can have democracy in this country or we can have great wealth concentrated in the hands of a few, but we can't have both.
—LOUIS BRANDEIS
Let each man pass his days in that wherein his skill is greatest.
—SEXTUS PROPERTIUS

David and I listen for the *click* that tells us lids are sealing on the new batch of canning, counting one, two, three . . . until all seven quarts are safely sealed. I line them up, admiring the golden half-globes of peaches neatly overlapping like shingles on a roof. My chest fills and I feel smile muscles contracting, reminding me of how my mother used to look, gazing at the beautiful jars of newly canned fruit and vegetables. It's the way I feel when the garden is growing well and finally (semi) tidy. The way I used to feel at the end of a half marathon. Or a marathon. The way I felt when I held my first published book. It's the glow of accomplishment earned by hard work. It seems to me that's a lot of what life is about—doing things you love, things that take some effort, things that make you feel good.

In the United States, we say we honor individualism, personal rights, and freedoms, but what do we do to help develop those values? How many schools offer programs that cultivate a student's unique talents? More often they seem to be cutting or de-emphasizing art, music, philosophy, and critical and creative thinking in deference to job training—training frequently for do-as-you're-told, don't-ask-questions jobs that may, by the time of graduation, be gone, shipped overseas or done by robots. Increasingly, politicians and media commentators seem to judge education by its preparation for jobs and judge leaders of opposing parties by their production of jobs. The job is the thing, not its potential for personal satisfaction or its value to society.

Skyrocketing diabetes rates create more jobs in hospitals and the pharmaceutical industry. Oil spills and natural disasters mean jobs in cleanup and rescue. Prisons and wars provide jobs. We cheer the rising GDP, not asking what is happening to our world and our society.

But life costs money, you say. We need a job, any job, to buy what we have no time to grow or can or make because we're too busy working. We want a job for its purchasing power rather than its potential for developing our talents so that our work gives some satisfaction. We seem not to consider living on less so that we don't have to work more than we want to.

When I had an appointment at the hospital recently, the echocardiogram technician effervesced about her chosen life's work. She found diagnostic analysis endlessly fascinating. She felt thrilled with what she was doing and how she imagined the future, and she felt doubly lucky compared to some of her colleagues who complained that they hated their jobs. Still, that confused her. She wanted to tell them, if there is no way to enjoy it, why not find something else? This is your life! Listening to her, I thought of the Kahlil Gibran quote: "Work is love made visible."

Yet the harder that jobs are to find, the more frightened and desperate we become because we have to eat or pay the rent or have/do at least what the neighbor has and does, and chances are, we're already in debt. But where can we find that feeling of accomplishment, if we are wage slaves?

April 2011 was the 150th anniversary of the beginning of the Civil War, with reenactments, films, and analysis filling the papers and airwaves. Some of the commentary reminded listeners of our nation's need to find "our better angels," to rid ourselves of prejudice, to confront inequality. My great-grandfather fought in the Civil War, but I was nearly thirty before the Civil Rights Act was passed. A century later! Clearly, things have improved, though slowly. But by how much?

Confederates had slaves to work the plantations so the plantation owner could maintain his lifestyle. Fast forward to find people living in company towns, working for the company. The workers were not slaves; they were paid for their labors. They rented their homes from the company and bought provisions from the company store—frequently requiring more than their paycheck could cover. But they were given credit, becoming ever more indebted. So didn't the company own them?

Now low-wage citizens and undocumented immigrants grow our food, care for our children, our elderly, our homes, our gardens; they clean hotel rooms, build roads and houses. Mid-wage folks work multiple jobs, often boring or repetitive or demeaning, so they have no time to know their children or explore their unique interests, no feeling of fulfillment in employment. They work two jobs because they are paid too poorly to buy what corporate advertisement has convinced them they need. They must borrow from the corporate banks to buy from the corporate stores and make payments with interest to the corporations, who profit handsomely. They work because they are consumers, and consumption requires money. They are worked because their employer is a consumer, and perhaps is evolving into a wood rat or bowerbird. Or perhaps needs more to buy more companies, to buy more people, to buy more nests, to be the biggest wood rat of them all.

Oracle's CEO Larry Ellison is said to have proclaimed, "It is not sufficient that I succeed; Everyone else must fail," a quote attributed originally to Genghis Khan or Attila the Hun, among others. This might be the battle cry of capitalism and the free market system, which seem to *require* winners and losers. Low wages and a certain amount of unemployment are necessary for the bottom line to pencil out—the bottom line being profit for the CEO and the shareholders.

According to some biologists and anthropologists, the greed, competition, and violence concomitant with capitalism are part of human nature. It is how we evolved to the successful species we have become. E. O. Wilson says our bloody nature helped civilize us as we formed competitive groups for hunting or building or protection. As a tribe formed families, gardens, or good hunting grounds, they had to fight to maintain them.

Perhaps it is true that violence and greed helped our upward evolution, but what about that drive to form family, or building or hunting groups? Those require mutual understanding and cooperation. I wonder if now, when so much of humankind is suffering and the planet itself is threatened by our "success," it isn't time for us to use our storied intelligence to look into the more compassionate and cooperative aspects of our nature and find another model. My American dream is that we can do work that is fulfilling, that is done because it gives us joy. That we are able to provide for ourselves or cooperate in community sufficiently to lose our fear of being without (money, food, respect, health), so we don't feel a need to acquire (more, more, more). That our nation's economy is not based on growth, because endless growth is a cancer, devouring its host. We cannot continue to grow. We cannot create more water, soil, minerals, or old growth in the next business cycle. If society persists in accepting that success is measured in accumulation of wealth and the trophies that advertise that accumulation, and continues to accept an economic system built on most of us working for the good of very few of us—fueled by the fiction that each citizen can become queen if she is a good little worker bee—then as resources become scarcer and wages for all but the elite become lower, bitterness, anger, depression, and violence are sure to follow.

My friend Stephanie posted a photo on her Facebook page of a group of African children sitting in a circle, their legs straight in front of them like the spokes on a wheel. An anthropologist introduced them to a game. He would put a basket of candies under a nearby tree and when he gave the signal, whoever reached it first could have all of the candies. The children watched excitedly. As he placed the basket and gave a whistle, they dashed to the tree, holding hands. All arrived together; all shared the candy.

The anthropologist asked why no one had tried to win the prize.

"It's Ubuntu," the children replied. "How could one of us be happy if all of the others are sad?"

Perhaps this story is only a parable. But parable or not, it is a clear illustration of a philosophy of life. Ubuntu expresses the essence of being human, explains Bishop Tutu. I am what I am because of who we all are. Humans don't and can't exist in isolation and what we do affects the whole world. Ubuntu speaks of our interconnectedness, so beautifully symbolized by the picture of all of those children forming one big circle—a wheel of empathy, a wheel of cooperation.

For the past couple of decades a group of scientists has collaborated with the Dalai Lama and several other Buddhist scholars in a series of workshops on the Mind and Life. At the eighth round, in March of 2000, the Dalai Lama wanted a scientific perspective on the brain's responses to destructive emotions, defined as those causing harm to the self, including addictive cravings, paralyzing fear, and hatred. (I would argue that the fear of doing without and stress to beat out the other guy would also be considered destructive.) The scientists explored how negative emotions eat away at both thought processes and function, actually changing the shape and size of the prefrontal lobes. They also reported on brain scans performed on Buddhist scholars during meditation and charted links between disciplined mental strategies and their effect on brain function. Over and over they observed the neuroplasticity of the brain and its ability to change and develop through life.

The Dalai Lama and the scientists discussed how children might be taught to live with full attention and self-awareness, learning emotional self-management and fostering compassion and love for all beings. What would it be like if in our homes and schools, children and their parents practiced recognizing emotions in themselves and others and managing their own emotions? The workshop attendees agreed that such practice could decrease violence, depression, and other problems arising from "afflictive emotions."

Society has seen addicts turn around their behavior—something taking tremendous effort founded in deep desire for change coupled with disciplined practice. Not only addiction to drugs and alcohol, but addiction to wealth, to power, or to adulation could be overcome with an understanding of the insecurities that drive those hungers, along with determination to live differently. Having experienced in my own life the changes possible when you understand what you're feeling, rather than just react to it, I find this an exciting prospect. Being able to recognize when it's our lizard brain—the amygdala, that primitive part of the brain that tells us to be afraid or to fight or to mate—that is being stimulated by what another person says or does, or what we hear on the television or radio, or what we read, can alert us to when we are letting ourselves be manipulated. We can learn to spot the opportunity to shift gears and use the thinking part of our brains. We can be rational if we take the *self* out of the equation, if we realize it's not all about me. We can learn empathy and compassion.

My cousin Joan told me a story about two little boys she overheard confirming to each other that they were "best friends. And best friends share lice." Pretty cute! But how about best friends sharing feelings? Might sharing feelings make friends out of enemies? If we learn how to recognize our feelings, and see ourselves (or our sons, daughters, mothers, fathers, loved ones) in others, will we still choose to exploit or impoverish or kill them?

With understanding of our mutual needs and the security of acceptance, we would be freer to pursue our uniqueness. Not everyone can be a Shakespeare, a Beethoven, a Picasso, or a Steve Jobs, but everyone has interests and talents. Some of those have been seriously squelched at home or school, but they are still there, however deeply buried. Why should we stand in line, hat in hand, for someone to pay us for doing boring work so that the boss can get rich? Let the boss hire a robot and that worker do what she loves. Maybe I'm not able to be an independent contractor, a self-starter, an organizer. But some of us are and we can join with others, use all of our talents, feel that glow of accomplishment. Ayn Rand and her present-day disciples speak of the "fight for individualism versus collectivism," but that seems like an irrational choice. I would vote to develop both. Each beautiful individual drop of water join with its fellows to make a river. It takes lovely and strong individual threads to make a stunning tapestry. Our most realized selves, working in concert, can create the most fulfilling future for us all and for our progeny.

A spacecraft named Dawn has been exploring the asteroid Vesta for about a year and soon will begin a two-and-a half-year journey to Ceres, the other large asteroid in the belt between Mars and Jupiter. Dawn made the 1.7 billion mile trip to Vesta and will add another nine hundred million miles to Ceres powered by ion propulsion, which seems to me like something out of a science fiction film. Electric fields accelerate a beam of positively charged xenon gas ions that are expelled at speeds up to ninety thousand mph. Two solar panels provide the energy to accelerate the xenon. In the past, spacecraft, like automobiles, have had to carry the necessary fuel on board, greatly increasing the weight of the craft and limiting the distance traveled. While conventional spacecraft would have to have carried 2.5 tons of fuel to reach Vesta, Dawn carried only 937 pounds of xenon, and still has enough on board to get to Ceres, as the sun recharges the craft's panels for the energy necessary for propulsion.

So why can't we use some of this technology on Earth? Just imagine. Solar-powered electric vehicles delivering us to solar-powered mass transit with ion engines. Sewage whisked away to central solar and ion-powered composters and whisked back as compost to community or private gardens. How about smart-phone apps that sense when we are low on a particular nutrient or will suggest a therapy program for an ailment or weakness? Or a communication device that notifies us when our particular skills are needed or some of our needs are available in the neighborhood?

Human intelligence and ingenuity are facts. If our schools and systems—social, political, economic—are geared toward developing individual potential at the same time that people recognize our total interdependency, both on each other and on a healthy, intact, diverse natural world, we are bright enough to save this battered planet at the same time that we live in joy, doing what we do best. Big in the news is job loss due to the proliferation and sophistication of technology. In the near future, we probably will no longer be able to find those mid-wage routine jobs that used to be so necessary and that were hated by so many. So now is the time, rather than to bemoan joblessness, to do what we've always wanted to do. Start our own business. Form a co-op. Join together. Take care of each other. But if we see the bottom line in dollar signs for the GDP rather than in health and happiness, we'll end up with a few well-feathered nests amidst great misery.

I truly believe such an enormous turnabout could happen, but I think it will require some basic changes. Like the house that is built on a strong foundation, society must be built from the bottom up, built by people working together, not content to wait for action from above any more than the plants, insects, and microorganisms would wait for the top predators to initiate action. We need the courage to accept responsibility for our own happiness and, at the same time, to have compassion for those in need. If we have enough self-respect to see who we are and what gives us joy, we can see how best to contribute to society. Once we are true to ourselves, we can learn how to network—how to help, rather than compete with each other. And then we must realize that we are indeed consumers, completely dependent on the gifts of the earth. If we acknowledge that, how could we not prioritize the health of this planet, the wellspring of our very being, rather than being number one? It doesn't seem like such a radical goal, being personally fulfilled and while we're at it, saving the planet for our great grandchildren.

What is life all about? Is it doing what we enjoy, improving the world, and feeling gratified, or is it stress and panic and competing to get all of the candies? Is it winners and losers, or is it Ubuntu?

25
Life's Winter

For life and death are one, even as the river and the sea are one.
——KAHLIL GIBRAN
Keep cool: it will be all one a hundred years hence.
——RALPH WALDO EMERSON

December 9, 2010. Cold, dark, slippery with mud and drenching wet; leaf-less trees, dead plants, wind whipping through my ears and into my bones. Winter. What's to love? I have entered the winter of my life, and spring will not return. No wonder seniors get depressed.

"Make the best of it," my mother would have said. So I search for whatever "best" might be hiding beneath the muck and ice.

Before me is an old oak tree. Its gnarly branches, covered with moss and lichen, would have looked dead to my father, but in its wood, that oak carries the sun and rain and minerals of its many years. Tiny buds on its branches store potential born the past growing season. On the ground its leaves decay, giving homes to insect eggs, food for slugs, millipedes and a myriad of soil organisms, all of which will eventually make a marvelous mix to become new soil. The oak roots network with microorganisms, sharing stored sugar and receiving minerals and water. The old tree, like the hidden tiger lilies, the mules' ears, and the fescue, has invested its year's energies in seeds that, now scattered about, will gather moisture from winter's soil to swell embryos waiting inside their seed coats for their turn at life. The oak tree doesn't mourn the winter, but profits from what it has stored, networking and broadcasting its riches.

Meanwhile, hunkered down and out of sight, countless individuals quietly thrive. Rhizomes, bulbs, insect pupae, snoozing black bears, and jumping mice continue to change and grow during the cold dark days. Juncos, finches, nuthatches, chipmunks, and squirrels seem, if anything, to pick up their tempo of life, perhaps needing to work triple-time to get their jobs done in the limited light. Winter is the most productive season for the woodland fungi, now pushing mushrooms through the soil to spread their spores, and for licorice fern, flourishing in dense colonies on the branches of maple and oak trees. And it is now that owls call for their mates and whales launch their long journey to warmer waters.

Winter's low-angled light illumines objects in uncommon ways, perhaps allowing new discoveries. And winter is the season of growing light, each day brighter than the last, each day bathed longer in the climbing sun's illumination. A season of such promise is neither dreary nor depressing.

So in this, the winter of my life, may my leaves also nourish the soil; may I divine the secret of continuing to grow in the dark; may I remember to network and share and to nurture the embryos of whatever viable seeds I have been able to disseminate. May I always search through the mud for its source: life-giving water. May I ever be guided by the steady waxing of the light, and may I also, like the bears, seek the peace and contentment of rest.

Winter. I aim to exploit its potential. But still, as I lie skin-to-skin beside my husband, his hands remembering the contours of my body, my eyes prickle with the knowledge that while the opportunities seem endless, the season is not. Yet another reminder to hold close the moment, drink deeply of its liquor, breathe in its essence. Today is all that is.

And someday my todays will be over. When I plan habitat for creatures— reptiles, amphibians, birds, bugs—I think of the whole life cycle. What do they need for egg laying? Where will the young be raised? What will they eat at each stage of their lives? How will they die? Will they nourish some other creature?

I saw a western tanager sitting on a fence wire in my garden. I've seen them flying here, seen them in a cherry tree, nibbling fruit, even seen them swooping to catch insects—a meal on the wing. But I had never seen one so close or so still. This was a male—its beautiful scarlet head suffused to a sunset peach at the throat; the gold body handsomely set off by black wings with white and gold markings, black back and tail. As I watched, he teetered slightly, then tumbled to the ground. He showed no sign of injury, but was clearly dead.

I wondered about the cause. Had he been poisoned? Was this a delayed reaction to some outwardly invisible injury—a concussion perhaps, from flying into a window? Did he have some awful bird disease that was now going to rip through whole populations? Or maybe it was just what the obituary section in the newspaper refers to as "age-related causes." My wonderings then shifted to the next step. Should I leave him there to be recycled by a scavenger, eaten, reprocessed by microorganisms, his nutrients returned to the soil? Or should I bury him and let the arthropods and microorganisms beneath the soil do the recycling? After some consideration, I opted for the latter. The more natural thing would have been to let him lie there, but I didn't want to watch or smell the process. It's my twentieth-century hang-ups, perhaps. I read about cultures that leave their dead on the rooftops to be devoured by raptors, and I get it. I appreciate that as an example of closing the circle of life. And I watched in spellbound fascination as the yellow jackets turned the vole to a meatless skeleton. Perhaps the tanager's beauty fires a different set of synapses in my brain, pushing scientific curiosity aside in favor of a more emotional response. As enamored as I am of the whole process of decomposition, sometimes I prefer it to happen well out of my field of vision.

As we build our house and I think about my larger home, I necessarily think about my own complete life cycle. I have long known that I didn't want to tie up land, waste money, and cause the pollution—particularly of embalming fluids finding their way to the groundwater—of conventional burial. I thought that instead, I would be cremated when I die. But though not nearly as costly as conventional burial, that too is expensive, and it has environmental impacts. With temperatures of about sixteen hundred to nearly eighteen hundred degrees Fahrenheit for one to two-and-a-half hours, cremation not only uses fossil fuels (natural gas, propane, or diesel), it also releases about 110 pounds of greenhouse gas per body, including nitrogen oxide, carbon monoxide, and sulfur dioxide. It is still a much more environmentally responsible choice than a fancy coffin in a concrete vault, with chemicals leaking out into the soil, but I thought I could do better. Ed Abbey had his friends haul his body out into the mountains and leave him there to be found by nature's scavengers. That gave me an idea.

With delight, I discover green burial is legal here in Oregon, and I can arrange to be buried on our own property. I've picked a spot near some oak trees. My preference would be to be wrapped in a shroud (or a sheet) and buried directly into the soil, but since I won't be doing the work, I'll defer to those who will. A cardboard box would be fine. Great grandchildren could paint flowers on it or poems or bon voyage messages. Or if they want something more substantial, a box could be pine, perhaps built by my progeny. What's important is that it doesn't pollute and will decay fast enough not to overly delay my return to the earth. It makes me feel good to think of fertilizing these beautiful woods. I will join the old oak tree, and in it, spring will come again. And I will be eternally home.

Along with money, decomposition, and body processes, death is a topic our culture tries to avoid. Ignore it, and maybe it will go away. I'm picturing the little child with hands over her eyes saying, "You can't see me!" But I wonder whether, if we thought about death as a natural stop on the carousel, we might live our lives differently. A T-shirt slogan I first read a decade or more ago reads, "He who dies with the most toys, still dies." In the game of life, there are no golden parachutes, no bailouts. The angel of death cannot be bought. The 1 percent is as sure of death as are the 99 percent.

December 9, 2012. I am now seventy-seven. Incredible! I remember when I thought thirty was old. Now I don't feel like seventy-seven is, except when I look in the mirror. I wonder if I would have believed it if someone long ago had told me that you don't get old inside. A bit tired sometimes, but I was at thirty, too.

In four days David and I will have been here in our woods twenty years. All of those seasons and creatures: fat, floating, golden maple leaves, new sticky spring buds, vegetables and voles, tents and trailer, brain hemorrhage and building a better nest, all has zoomed by, and yet it seems forever and always.

And now we are, unbelievably, seventy-seven, or so we are told, and I want very much to sit down and visit with my parents as peers. Mother just made it six weeks past seventy-five. I have another six weeks to go to reach Daddy's final age. Such an odd concept. You can't be the same age as, or older than, your parents. But here I am, just that.

I try to imagine what it would be like if they came to visit now. I can see their glowing faces, as delighted to get together as I am. Having known for over three-quarters of a century that my parents were without question the founts of all knowledge, I probably would ask their advice. And they probably wouldn't give it, believing as they did that we each should find our own way—albeit with an occasional hand or nudge if requested. Mother might quote the little Mother Goose ditty, "For every problem under the sun / there is a remedy or there is none. / If there is one, seek till you find it. / If there is none, never mind it."

But then they would turn the conversation back to me, an empowering and gratifying habit of theirs. They would love our woods, Daddy wanting to explore, Mother asking for stories about the animals and a list of the resident plants. I imagine they would notice we were without lawns or ornamental gardens, but they would not be judgmental. Rather, they probably would ask about our plans for constructing swales and rain gardens to slow the runoff and to clean gray water, making mini-wetland habitats. Mother would be sorry, but not surprised, that consumption and development seemed to be taking precedence over the environment in today's world. Fifty and more years ago she lamented that tendency. Daddy would wonder if nations were beginning to learn how to get along. I would be able to report that, although it still seems like people are squabbling—or attacking each other—most of the time, since the end of World War II, the rates of violent death have plummeted to the lowest level in recorded history. Political scientist Joshua Goldstein, who says we are winning the war on war, attributes that to the United Nations as well as other groups around the world who work for peace. My father would be pleased to hear that. A municipal court judge for years, convinced that reason, empathy, and the law could solve most problems, he came close to being appointed to a Washington State Supreme Court judgeship, a position he would have enjoyed. He believed—perhaps was told—that the sole thing standing in the way of the appointment was his advocacy for a world government, apparently considered a Communist idea then, or at least one not giving appropriate deference to American exceptionalism. It's a pity. He would have been a good judge, for the state or for the world.

I like thinking about us mid-seventy-year-olds sitting around the breakfast table having a chat. It has been thirty-two years since they walked their gardens, but their molecules still help the earth to flourish, and they are still very much with me—in my heart, my thoughts, my way of looking at things. Mother would approve my burial plans. After all, it was she who first taught me to recycle.

26

The Upper Floors

Never doubt that a small group of thoughtful, committed citizens
can change the world. Indeed, it is the only thing that ever has.
——MARGARET MEAD
Fear cannot be without hope nor hope without fear.
——BARUCH SPINOZA

It's 1:10 a.m. on Monday, August 22, 2011, the morning of our grandson Nate's twenty-seventh birthday. He's sleeping, perhaps, (or more likely, not yet) in Los Angeles, while I sit in a rocking chair in the waiting room of a birthing center in Springfield, Oregon, where our granddaughter Celina, Nate's sister, is hard at work to bring her first child into the world. The two men dearest to me on this planet, David and our son, Jeff, sleep nearby on couches probably chosen for that very purpose, as I read an essay about gratitude. Gratitude, the author says, is a way of life.

Just a day and a half ago, Jeff, the grandfather-to-be, survived a twenty-foot climbing fall, barely glanced by a boulder falling close behind him. It had been a rare unprogrammed sunny Saturday, the perfect opportunity to explore what some of his rock-climbing friends considered a prime climb. He travelled alone, so he would just look, and maybe clean a path for a later ascent, rather than climb. But the gully he came to before the climbing wall turned out to be deeper than it had first appeared, and rather than a scramble, it was a true climb. Jeff made his way up a crack, testing rock, spotting handholds, wedging feet. He shifted his weight to grab an air-conditioner-sized rock jutting out from the face. It was big, stable and reliable looking. He grasped it firmly—and it came loose. The boulder made a crater two feet deep and four feet square, about a foot beside where Jeff landed. His body seemed compressed—jammed—his legs and feet in trouble, but what?

Sprained? Broken? He couldn't stand, but he was alive. It took him five and a half hours to drag his beat-up body to his truck, just two miles away. He drove the old stick-shift Toyota by force of will, clutching with his right foot, sliding through stop signs. At the edge of town he called Rachel. They were separated, yet, although the relationship hadn't worked out, he had complete trust in her compassion and competence, and he needed help. The ER doctor found a broken rib, a badly sprained back, and severe bone bruising in his ankle, but—with a boot, crutches, and considerable pain—here he is at the birthing center to await his granddaughter. And I am grateful.

David sleeps with his hands clasped across his chest, yellow comb falling half out of brown jacket pocket, his diaphragm gently rising and falling. His curly graying hair recedes at the temples sufficiently that I can see part of the scar from the brain surgery he had more than sixteen years ago. This new life coming into the world—her mother struggling so hard to help her come—this tiny girl, this Evangeline, will have a strong determined mother, a patient supportive father, and a healthy granddaddy and great grampa to greet her, as they—we all—will have Celina and Geoffrey's new daughter to welcome into our hearts. How could I not be grateful? My cup overflows.

Celina vocalizes from deep in her body. It's apparent she has had voice training. And breath training too. Valuable tools, both. Her conservatory years are serving her well.

I take none of it for granted. People die from brain hemorrhages, from falls, from being smashed by boulders, from childbirth. My husband, our son, his daughter—our lives are a gift. We might never have been born, and once born, life might have been taken away. But it wasn't.

Two hours pass and Evangeline is still not ready to leave that warm dark place she has called home the past nine months. Celina's full contralto calls to her, ohms, low, low, sometimes climbing in an urgency to bring forth the babe, but still she waits. Hair tossing, body swaying *ah ah ahhhhh* to the beat of the body's rhythm. I want us all to join hands around Celina and *ohm ohm ohhmmmmm*. Chant the baby out.

Is the little one struggling, too, or just her mother? How many hours of work, labor without rest, walls pushing, undulating, preparing to expel their small passenger, how many hours can a woman endure? Contractions began at two o'clock yesterday afternoon—fourteen and a half hours so far.

Future grandmother Sara, mother of Geoffrey, the father-to-be, joins us and we all go down the hall to the homey birthing room. 5:31. For six and a half hours the contractions have been at two-minute intervals. Celina's water broke hours earlier. The midwife says we'll give it another couple hours and if there's no change, transfer to the hospital.

Now it's 7:30 and the contractions have slowed. The cervix won't dilate much past 5 cm. We move from the birthing center to the nearby hospital, arriving at a comfortable, welcoming room. Celina gets drugs to relax her body, to alleviate pain, to stimulate contractions, and to fight infection. I take David home to care for our granddog, Homer, and perhaps to get a bit of rest, then return as quickly as I can. At 9:30 they tell us that if things haven't improved in a couple of hours they'll schedule a C-section. The baby's heart monitor broadcasts her health and strength. *Babum babum babum.* No stress to worry about at this point. Mama will keep working.

11:30. 12:30. Doctors, nurses, midwife check blood pressure, temperature, contractions, dilation, baby's heart. Maybe. We'll see. No problems yet, just not much change. One p.m. marks twenty-four hours labor.

Four o'clock. Seven o'clock. So tired. Geoffrey naps. Celina tells the midwife, *I close my eyes between contractions.*

Eight o'clock and there's new action. Contractions are getting bigger and closer together. The cervix is dilated except for one spot. Nine o'clock, the midwife gives pushing instructions. At 9:20 Nate sends a text message. There's just two hours and forty minutes left of his birthday! Jeff texts back, *We'll make it!*

Celina lies at about a 45-degree angle, frog legged. Geoffrey holds her right knee and calf; Sara holds the left. When contractions come, they are to press the bent legs toward the body.

Take a deep breath, curl your head forward, push the breath out through your bottom, the midwife instructs Celina. Jeff helps support her head and shoulders.

Imagine a world-record discus- or hammer thrower. Hear him yell with an explosive throw. That is the sound of a healthy woman pushing out a baby. Power of a weight thrower, endurance of a marathon runner. Deep breath. Push it out. Over and over and over. Father, grand- and great-grandparents hovering, holding, pressing, cheering. *Go go go go! Good job!* Celina's skin flushes, glistens with the exertion. Perspiration beads up, then trickles down her temples. We get a cool washcloth for her brow, her cheeks, her neck, bits of ice for her to crunch between pushes. Jeff holds the phone near so that Celina's mother in New Mexico can be virtually present.

About two hundred mighty pushes, Jeff calculates, and look! There's the top of the head!

Wait till the next contraction, the midwife says.

Uuuuuuhhh!

The rest of the head! 10:35. One and a half hours of pushing; thirty-three and a half hours of labor. The midwife holds the baby's head and guides as Celina pushes out shoulders, chest. The baby wails. Celina's eyes go wide, fingers stretch, arms shoot out. *My baby*, she cries, as the feet pop out and she nestles Evangeline to her chest.

Tearily, I look around me and think, *Gratitude. What else?*

December 22, 2012. Evangeline is sixteen months old.

In house building, as we build the foundation, we must consider the needs of the upper floors. My house—my life—has a foundation strong and deep. But I wonder about the upper floors, my progeny. They are really where my focus lies. Erika, our professor daughter; her daughters Tasha, nearly sixteen, and Camila, pushing eleven; our son Jeff, teacher and coach; and his grown children Nate and Celina; Celina's daughter Evangeline and Evangeline's future siblings and cousins, their children's children. They, and all of their generations—what will they inherit? Have we, or the greater *we* that is our society, our Western civilization, knocked out so many concrete blocks that once the house is theirs it will crumble? Will mudslides wash it downhill to be buried in the muck? Will floods float it out to sea, the poor sea, already so full of our ill-conceived flotsam?

My children and grandchildren are strong, creative, resourceful, and responsible. They will all build homes to match their qualities. Even little Evangeline, now nearly a year and a half old, so inquisitive, adventurous and tough, will do a magnificent job of taking care of herself, I'm sure. But what I worry about is their larger home—the world over which they will have little control, the biosphere where they will build their houses and gardens.

We're supposed to want each generation to do better economically than the last, but while they might—and our children definitely are doing so—I wish for them health, clear rivers, old-growth forests, diverse species. I wish a world in peace with people unafraid, joining together. I wish them happiness in a sound and healthy world, their home. I wish them gratitude and joy; I wish them empathy and love.

The exciting thing is, I do see good things happening. Yes, the seas still will rise. Clearly we can't rapidly reduce the CO_2 in the air. There will definitely be negative and perhaps devastating effects. But people are getting it. They care. Increasingly, people are rejecting the corporate model in favor of cooperatives that acknowledge interdependency, provide equitable distribution of wealth, and give members a feeling of self-worth. People are banding together in myriad ways. Groups clean rivers and ocean shores. Others trek to the wilderness to remove fences that block or endanger the passage of animals. Citizens join each other online to change laws, proving that the people really do have a say in a democracy: it is not only corporations that can lobby the government. Social movements are where we have power, says activist Tim DeChristopher.

Citizen scientists use the Internet to solve problems cooperatively. One site, ResearchGate, is dedicated to sharing scientific research worldwide, inviting input and collaboration where once (and often still) such work was competitive and closely guarded. Just five years old, the site is now used by more than three million researchers. "We're Stronger Together," another site proclaims. Research, advocacy, employment, sustenance, we're stronger together. David and I recently visited a community garden where a dozen neighbors plan, plant, weed, and willingly share with others who are able to give less time. Best of all is the neighborhood compost pile where everyone contributes their kitchen scraps or garden clippings, covering each addition with a scoop of sawdust. The finished product adds to the cooperative garden.

In Shannon Elizabeth Bell's moving book, *Ironweed*, Appalachian women tell of their fight against the pollution and destruction of mountaintop removal. Together they were able to effect change, and doing so gave them a new sense of personal purpose and self worth. "I felt like a nobody . . . but now I feel like I can make a difference," one woman said. In several western states, environmental groups and industry, formerly dedicated foes, are discovering their common goals for resilient, sustainable ecosystems and are forming collaborative groups to map out plans that will address diverse needs. One collaborator called it an exercise in democracy. "The collaborative gives a voice that we never had." In research, advocacy, community work, outreach, employment, use of public resources, together we can make a difference, and joining together makes us feel better about ourselves and about the future. It's not just a dream; it's happening. The United Nations declared 2012 to be the International Year of the Cooperative, with one billion people—one in five adults over the age of fifteen—now co-op member-owners. And great multiples of that number join ranks in other ways.

I'm planning to put together a questionnaire for our neighborhood to assess what people see as their potential needs, or what services, skills, or supplies they could contribute toward a cooperative neighborhood community. Rural folks are famous for independence, so some may find it difficult to acknowledge needs. But they are quick to help others. Early in our time here, I slipped into a ditch one snowy day when I was backing our car out of a neighbor's driveway. Before I could wonder what to do, three young men had me back on the road. I don't even know who they were or which house they came from. But that spirit is prevalent in the country.

The neighborhood could have a community garden. Or help in each other's gardens. I once knew a group of gardeners who would take turns, all of them working together in each other's gardens. Together we could can our produce. It's far easier and way more fun when lots of people help. We could have a tool-lending library, saving money. Maybe someone would be good at senior or sick care. We could have an SOS system for contact in case of emergency. Or neighbors could volunteer to drive or run errands for one another, or just have a book club or regular potlucks to keep in contact. I once asked Mother how I would be able to pay her and Daddy back for all they had done through the years. She said, "You don't pay back. You pay forward." People sometimes move to town when they can no longer manage on their own in the country, but we could all stay longer—maybe forever—if we could help each other, if we would pay forward.

Maybe the Mayan calendar really did predict the end of the world—the world as we know it, that is. The end of the old way—the king-of-the-mountain way—and the beginning of caring about each other and about the planet that sustains us all. In the ecosystem, each organism has a role. Each plant, worm, and bug contributes to the function of the system. I would like to see a system where humans have as much opportunity as beetles or hummingbirds to contribute according to our unique abilities. We would each have the satisfaction of knowing we've done our part. We would have a reason to get up in the morning, knowing our role is an important one. Don't people deserve to be as useful as, say, ants? Working together, giving our best, being fulfilled, feeling grateful. That is the nest I want for my progeny.

I have a vision for their schools, too. Maybe it's time to add a fourth "R" to reading, 'riting and 'rithmetic: I propose a class in relations. It would have two sections: ecosystem and human. In the first, students would learn about the functioning and interdependency of the systems of the natural world and how our actions affect them and, in turn, affect all earthlings. The second section would focus on the functioning of the human brain, and how understanding our emotions can affect both our behavior and our compassion for others. Aren't these universal needs—to be a valuable part of a larger whole and to love both self and others?

On the south side of our house, where leaves fly in the wind and flurries of snow sporadically swirl, David and Geoffrey are framing the greenhouse. I'll be able to start my garden seeds there next season whatever the weather. No more excuse for a late start just because spring dawdles her way to our garden. I'll have a place to hang clothes to dry even when it rains, and when future winters roll around, there will be no more bathtub for the storms to fill.

But now, I must get back to the *inside* of my nest and to those upper floors (and the lower floors and the ceilings and the walls). This is the winter to finish the tiling and to accomplish that katydid-in-the-beard paint job. Then as the day fades and I am cozy in our well-insulated, wood-fire-warmed room with the beautiful myrtlewood floor, I hope I remember to send a special blessing to that fat-bellied, apple-thieving bear, snuggled down in its winter bed. He stole nearly the entire winter's apple harvest, destroyed one tree, and beat up some others, and I'll do everything in my power to outwit him next year. But for a reason that I can't explain, I have a warm, indulgent, almost motherly feeling toward him.